WHY IS CHRISTMAS ON DECEMBER 25?

Dr. Maxwell Shimba

Shimba Publishing, LLC.

Shimba Theological Institute
United States of America

TABLE OF CONTENTS

INTRODUCTION

For the very first time, the celebration of Christmas was done by angels.

It is important for each of us to understand that the first to celebrate the birth of Jesus (Christmas) were God's holy angels.

(Luke 2:8-15) 8 And there were shepherds living out in the fields nearby, keeping watch over their flocks at night.
9 An angel of the Lord appeared to them, and the glory of the Lord shone around them, and they were terrified. 10 But the angel said to them, "Do not be afraid. I bring you good news that will cause great joy for all the people. 11 Today in the town of David a Savior has been born to you; he is the Messiah, the Lord. 12 This will be a sign to you: You will find a baby wrapped in cloths and lying in a manger."
13 Suddenly a great company of the heavenly host appeared with the angel, praising God and saying, 14 "Glory to God in the highest heaven, and on earth peace to those on whom his favor rests." 15 When the angels had left them and gone into heaven, the shepherds said to one another, "Let's go to

Bethlehem and see this thing that has happened, which the Lord has told us about.

Since God's holy angels celebrated the birth of Jesus, it is not a sin for anyone to celebrate Jesus' birth. These angels descended from heaven, praising God for the event of Jesus Christ's birth. If God's angels praised Him, you and I must also praise Him, as the angels' praise clearly indicates that this event was accepted by God.

Not only that, but the angels also declared that the birth of Jesus is "good news of great joy for all people."

This means that every human being should celebrate Jesus' birth, and that birth should bring them joy. Since this great joy is said to be for all people, it implies that anyone called a human being should share in this joy. If someone does not rejoice at Jesus' birth, they are likely not human but perhaps a spirit (demon), for a demon cannot be joyful about Jesus' birth, as His coming strips them of the power to torment people.

Now let me remind you of the meaning of Christmas:
The word "Christmas" comes from *Christ* and *Mass*, which when combined form the word *Christmas*, meaning "the worship of Christ."

This worship of Christ on earth officially began when Jesus was born, and the first to conduct this worship were the angels (Luke 2:13). The angels rejoiced and praised God for the birth of Christ. Therefore, if the angels praised God for Christ's birth and performed the first act of worship on earth — the worship of Christ, which in English is *Christmas* — we too must do the same. Any act performed by God's holy angels is undoubtedly sacred. Thus, when a person celebrates Jesus' birth, they perform a sacred act that pleases God.

The Wise Men Fell and Worshiped Jesus

Matthew 2:10-11 "When they saw the star, they were overjoyed. On coming to the house, they saw the child with his mother Mary, and they bowed down and worshiped him. Then they opened their treasures and presented him with gifts of gold, frankincense, and myrrh."

According to the Bible, these men known as the Wise Men came from "the East," and they learned of Jesus' birth while still in their homeland (Matthew 2:1-2, 9). It must have taken them a long time to travel from there to Judea. Finally, when they found Jesus, they fell and worshiped Him (Matthew 2:11).

Matthew 2:1-2 "After Jesus was born in Bethlehem in Judea, during the time of King Herod, Magi from the East came to Jerusalem and asked, 'Where is the one who has been born king of the Jews? We saw his star when it rose and have come to worship him.'"

The only one worthy of worship and reverence is God alone. So why did these astrologers and wise men from the distant East bow down and worship Jesus?

Why was King Herod troubled when he heard this, and why was all of Jerusalem disturbed along with him?

DR. MAXWELL SHIMBA

PART I

ORIGIN OF CHRISTMAS

CHAPTER 01

WHAT DOES CHRISTMAS MEAN?

In this first chapter, we will learn about:
i. The meaning of Christmas.
ii. The history of Christmas and December 25.
iii. The importance of Christmas history.
iv. Biblical reasons why Christians celebrate the Christmas holiday.

Key Verses to Remember:

Luke 2:9-11: "An angel of the Lord appeared to them, and the glory of the Lord shone around them, and they were terrified. But the angel said to them, 'Do not be afraid. I bring you good news that will cause great joy for all the people. Today in the town of David, a Savior has been born to you; He is the Messiah, the Lord.'"

Psalm 118:22-24: "The stone the builders rejected has become the cornerstone; the Lord has done this, and it is marvelous in our eyes. This is the day the Lord has made; we will rejoice and be glad in it." **Amen!**

---

i. The Meaning of Christmas:

CHRISTMAS (also *Noel*) is a holiday celebrated by many Christians to commemorate the birth of the Savior Jesus Christ more than 2,000 years ago on earth.

It is commonly celebrated on December 25 in Western Christianity and January 6 in Eastern or Orthodox Christianity.

There are two common names for this holiday:

Christmas: This word comes from the English term *Christ's Mass,* meaning the mass or worship of Christ.

Noel: This term comes from the English word *Noel* (or *Nowell*), borrowed from the French word *Noël,* which originates from the Latin *Natalis (dies),* meaning "(the day of) birth."

The Worship and Celebration of Jesus' Birth Is Biblical:

This is not something fabricated by certain individuals. Absolutely not! It is a biblical event established by God Himself.

The first act of worship and celebration of Jesus Christ's birth took place when He was born. The first to celebrate

His birth were the hosts of God's angels. Additionally, human beings also praised and glorified God for the birth of the Savior, Jesus Christ. Therefore, the concept of Christmas is biblical. (See Luke 2:7-14, 20, 25-38).

---

ii. The History of Christmas and December 25

The exact date of Jesus' birth is unknown because the Jewish culture of that time did not celebrate or commemorate birthdays.

However, as Christianity spread throughout the Roman Empire among nations accustomed to observing birthdays, the desire to celebrate the birth of the Savior, Christ, also emerged. This is the origin of the Christmas holiday.

Since the early 3rd century AD, various writers have discussed the date of Jesus Christ's birth.

The earliest recorded estimates of Jesus' birthdate come from Egypt around the year 200 AD.

The Christian writer Clement of Alexandria complained about the curiosity of some Egyptian scholars who claimed to have calculated the date in May, while others suggested April.

He also noted that a Christian group of Basilides' followers in Egypt celebrated Epiphany along with Jesus' birth on January 6.

Perhaps the estimate of December 25 also originated in Egypt. Beginning around the year 200 AD (mentioned for the first time in the writings of Sextus Julius Africanus), we learn that Egyptian scholars believed March 25 was the date of Christ's death and also the day of His conception. Adding nine months of pregnancy, December 25 emerged as the birthdate.

It seems that December 25 gained recognition around this time. A record from 204 AD by Hippolytus of Rome indicates that December 25 was celebrated as the birthdate of Jesus Christ.

Christmas and the Feast of Sol Invictus

Various scholars have claimed that the Church placed Christ's feast on that date to replace the feast of the sun god "Sol Invictus" (meaning "Unconquered Sun").

However, it is possible that events unfolded differently— that the emperors established the sun festival first and later scheduled it on December 25 to compete with Christianity, which was still under government persecution but continued to spread.

The one who introduced the "Birth of the Sun" (Mithra) feast in Rome was Emperor Elagabalus (reigned from 218 to 222). Later, Emperor Aurelian officially confirmed it in 273 AD, eventually moving it to December 25.

During the reign of Emperor Licinius (308-324 AD), the feast was still celebrated on December 19.

Catholic writer Mario Righetti candidly admitted that "to facilitate the acceptance of the Christian faith among pagans, the Church of Rome (under Emperor Constantine, who converted and was baptized as a Christian) transformed the pagan feast honoring the 'Invincible Sun' Mithra, the conqueror of darkness, into the celebration of Jesus Christ's birth on December 25."

(Reference: *History of the Liturgical Guide*, 1955, Vol. 2, p. 67).

From Rome, the capital of the Roman Empire, the December 25 celebration spread throughout Christianity.

Many Christians celebrate December 25 (Catholics, some Protestants, and Orthodox Christians). Among the Orthodox, other dates are also observed, particularly January 6, due to differences in calendars.

iii. The Importance of the History of Christmas

Let's consider some key points about Christmas:

1. If December 25 was originally a pagan festival, but later transformed into a celebration of Jesus Christ's birth,
This is perfectly acceptable before God. The Holy Spirit used the Roman Church under Emperor Constantine to change the existing pagan festival into Christmas.

This act is like bringing someone out of darkness into true light—leading them from the wrong path to the right and true way.

There's no issue with December 25 being transformed from a pagan celebration into a feast celebrating Jesus Christ's birth (Christmas). This change is entirely appropriate.

For example, the Bible speaks about this transformation in Acts 26:16-18:

"The Lord said to me, 'I am Jesus... But rise and stand on your feet; for I have appeared to you for this purpose, to make you a minister and a witness both of the things which you have seen and of the things which I will yet reveal to you. I will deliver you from your people and from the Gentiles, to whom I now send you, to open their eyes, to turn them from darkness to light, and from the power of Satan to God, that they may receive forgiveness of sins and an inheritance among those who are sanctified by faith in Me.'"

2. All Days Belong to God—There Is No Day for Satan.

Anyone who opposes the celebration of Christmas, claiming that December 25 was once a pagan holiday, misunderstands the matter. Such a person lacks spiritual understanding and misleads themselves.

It is crucial to understand that every day belongs to God—there is no day designated for Satan. It depends entirely on how an individual chooses to use the day—either to please God or to engage in ungodly deeds. There is no "special day" for Satan. All days belong to God, and He desires us to use every day to praise, worship, glorify, and please Him.

For example, the Bible emphasizes this in the following verses:

- **Genesis 1:14:** *"Then God said, 'Let there be lights in the firmament of the heavens to divide the day from the night; and let them be for signs and seasons, and for days and years.'"*
- **Psalm 105:4:** *"Seek the Lord and His strength; seek His face evermore."*
- **John 8:29:** *"And He who sent Me is with Me. The Father has not left Me alone, for I always do those things that please Him."*
- **Acts 2:46-47:** *"So continuing daily with one accord in the temple... praising God and having favor with all the people. And the Lord added to the church daily those who were being saved."*

As you can see, let us not give any day to Satan. Every day belongs to God because He created them. What remains is how each individual uses the day—whether to fulfill God's will or to engage in ungodly acts.

And with that understanding, if December 25 was once a pagan holiday, it was due to the misguided hearts of pagans who chose to use that day for their pagan practices. However, that does not mean December 25 inherently belongs to pagans. Absolutely not! It would only be pagan to us Christians if we participated in their pagan practices as they did. But if we use the day differently, it is no longer a pagan day but a holy day unto the Lord.

For us Christians who are saved, December 25 is a special day set apart to honor the Lord by remembering the great event of the birth of Jesus Christ, the Savior of the world.

The Bible says in **Romans 14:4, 6-7:** *"Who are you to judge another's servant? To his own master he stands or falls. Indeed, he will be made to stand, for God is able to make him stand. He who observes the day, observes it to the Lord; and he who does not observe the day, to the Lord he does not observe it. He who eats, eats to the Lord, for he gives God thanks; and he who does not eat, to the Lord he does not eat, and gives God thanks. For none of us lives to himself, and no one dies to himself."*

On December 25, we Christians use the day to honor the Lord. It is a special and unique day for Christians to reflect on the greatness of our God and His love for humanity. We rejoice, praise, glorify, sing, and give thanks to God our Father and our Savior Jesus Christ, who came to heal, save, and redeem humanity from the prison of Satan.

"This is a faithful saying and worthy of all acceptance, that Christ Jesus came into the world to save sinners, of whom I am chief."

(John 3:16-17; Luke 2:28-34; 1 Timothy 1:15-16)

If people can celebrate their birthdays and give thanks to God, how much greater and more meaningful it is to remember and celebrate the birth of our Savior Jesus Christ!

(3) We Do Not Celebrate a Date but the Memory of Our Savior's Birth into the World

The Bible says:

John 21:25: *"And there are also many other things that Jesus did, which if they were written one by one, I suppose that even the world itself could not contain the books that would be written. But these are written so that you may believe that Jesus is the Christ, the Son of God, and that by believing you may have life in His name."*

What does this mean?

Although the exact date and month of Jesus Christ's birth are unknown and not written in the Bible, that is not the important point. Before God, the specific date of Jesus' birth is not what matters; what matters is the event of His birth, which is why God chose to have it written down.

Many things Jesus did were not recorded, but His birth was documented because God wants us to understand that this event is essential and worth reflecting on. Knowing the exact date is not crucial for us, just as it wasn't for God. What matters is that Jesus Christ was born.

I emphasize again: the key point is not the specific date but the fact that Jesus Christ was born into the world. This is why we Christians celebrate not the date, but the memory of the event of His birth.

Even beyond December 25, at all times and in every season, we should celebrate and remember the birth of our Savior, Jesus Christ.

The Bible says in **Matthew 28:20:** *"...teaching them to observe all things that I have commanded you; and lo, I am with you always, even to the end of the age."*

Therefore, even as we celebrate His birth on December 25, Jesus is still with us.

iv. Biblical Reasons Why Christians Celebrate Christmas

The reasons are as follows:

(1) It Is a Divine Announcement Delivered by an Angel

The Bible says in **Luke 2:10-14:** *"But the angel said to them, 'Do not be afraid. I bring you good news that will cause great joy for all the people. Today in the town of David a Savior has been born to you; He is the Messiah, the Lord. This will be a sign to you: You will find a baby wrapped in cloths and lying in a manger.' Suddenly a great company of the heavenly host appeared with the angel, praising God and saying, 'Glory to God in the highest heaven, and on earth peace to those on whom His favor rests.'"*

You can see that even the multitude of heavenly angels joined with humans to rejoice and celebrate the birth of Jesus Christ.

Isaiah 9:6-7: *"For to us a child is born, to us a son is given, and the government will be on His shoulders. And He will be called Wonderful Counselor, Mighty God, Everlasting Father, Prince of Peace..."*

Anyone opposing the celebration of Christmas is likely influenced by a spirit of opposition from the enemy, possibly without realizing it.

---

(2) It Is a Biblical Command to Rejoice and Be Glad (on Christmas Day)

The Bible says in **Psalm 118:22-24:** *"The stone the builders rejected has become the cornerstone; the Lord has done this, and it is marvelous in our eyes. The Lord has done it this very day; let us rejoice today and be glad."*

The "cornerstone" mentioned here refers to Jesus Christ (**Ephesians 2:20**), and the "day" referred to is the day of His birth—Christmas!

The Bible also says in **Psalm 70:4:** *"May all who seek You rejoice and be glad in You; may those who long for Your saving help always say, 'The Lord is great!'"*

When Jesus Christ was born, He became the salvation of our God (**Luke 2:27-32; 1 Corinthians 1:30**). This is why Christians celebrate Christmas with joy and gladness, rejoicing in the birth of our Savior, Jesus Christ, who brought us salvation. Hallelujah!

(3) Celebrating Christmas Is Neither Sinful nor Wrong but God's Will for Us

The Bible says in **1 Corinthians 10:31:** *"So whether you eat or drink or whatever you do, do it all for the glory of God."*

Colossians 3:17: *"And whatever you do, whether in word or deed, do it all in the name of the Lord Jesus, giving thanks to God the Father through Him."*

This is why Christmas, beyond being a celebration, is also a special and unique day when many good deeds are done to give God praise, honor, glory, and abundant thanksgiving among saved Christians. God also manifests Himself in a special way on this day by healing, saving, touching, and visiting many people.

(4) The New Moon Festival Is a Foreshadowing of Jesus Christ's Birth Celebration

During the Old Testament times, people were commanded to celebrate the New Moon Festival as soon as the new moon appeared. They rejoiced and celebrated.

The Bible says in **Psalm 81:3-4:** *"Sound the ram's horn at the New Moon, and when the moon is full, on the day of our festival; this is a decree for Israel, an ordinance of the God of Jacob."*

It is important to understand that the New Moon Festival was a symbol, representation, or foreshadowing of the coming of Jesus Christ.

The Bible says in **Colossians 2:16-17:** *"Therefore do not let anyone judge you by what you eat or drink, or with regard to a religious festival, a New Moon celebration or a Sabbath day. These are a shadow of the things that were to come; the reality, however, is found in Christ."*

Now, Jesus Christ is the true Light of the world.

The Bible tells us in **John 8:12:** *"When Jesus spoke again to the people, He said, 'I am the Light of the world. Whoever follows Me will never walk in darkness but will have the Light of life.'"* (See also **John 1:9-10.**)

When Jesus Christ, the true Light, was born into this dark world, it was like a small light breaking forth and beginning to shine in the darkness.

Thus, just as the people of the Old Testament celebrated the New Moon Festival, that event was merely a foreshadowing of the celebration of Jesus Christ's birth that we celebrate today. Hallelujah!

(5) We Celebrate Christmas Because Jesus Christ Came So That We May Have Life and Have It Abundantly

The Bible says in **John 10:10:** *"The thief (Satan) comes only to steal and kill and destroy; I have come that they may have life, and have it to the full."*

Before Jesus Christ came into the world through His birth, Satan oppressed, tormented, and killed us without any help or deliverance.

But through Jesus Christ's coming into the world, He came to heal, save, and set us free from sin and the bondage of Satan. Everyone who calls on the name of the Lord receives healing and salvation.

Acts 10:38: *"How God anointed Jesus of Nazareth with the Holy Spirit and power, and how He went around doing good and healing all who were under the power of the devil, because God was with Him."*

Luke 9:1-2: *"When Jesus had called the Twelve together, He gave them power and authority to drive out all demons and to cure diseases, and He sent them out to proclaim the kingdom of God and to heal the sick."*

(See also **Luke 10:17-19.**)

If Jesus had not been born into the world, we would not have life, healing, or salvation.

But thanks be to God the Father, for through Jesus Christ's birth, we have been given power and authority. We have been healed and set free from all the chains of the devil.

Colossians 1:12-14: *"And giving joyful thanks to the Father, who has qualified you to share in the inheritance of His holy people in the kingdom of light. For He has rescued us from the dominion of darkness and brought us into the kingdom of the Son He loves, in whom we have redemption, the forgiveness of sins."*

(6) We Celebrate Christmas Because Jesus Christ's Birth Brought Hope to All Nations

Through Jesus Christ's birth, all nations outside of Israel, who once had no hope or God in the world, have been counted as part of God's inheritance.

Originally, God's chosen people were the Israelites, His people under the covenant with Jehovah. We, the other nations, were without hope and without God in the world, destined for eternal separation from Him.

Had Jesus Christ not been born, all nations outside of Israel would have remained alienated from God forever.

But through His birth, we have been reconciled with Israel and made one family as children of God. There is no distinction between Jew and Gentile.

The Bible says in **Ephesians 2:11-21, Galatians 3:26-29, and 1 Peter 2:5-10.**

NB:

These are the main biblical reasons why Christians celebrate Christmas.

Deciding to Celebrate Christmas or Not Is Not a Sin

There is no Scripture that forbids celebrating Christmas, nor is there a law in the Bible that mandates it.

Therefore, if you choose to celebrate Christmas for the glory of God, that's good. If you personally do not feel like celebrating Christmas, that's also fine!

The key point is that we should not argue, point fingers, or judge one another over the issue of Christmas. Let everyone exercise their faith freely, as long as they are not committing sin.

Romans 14:10-13, 19: *"You, then, why do you judge your brother or sister? Or why do you treat them with contempt? For we will all stand before God's judgment seat. It is written: 'As surely as I live,' says the Lord, 'every knee will bow before me; every tongue will acknowledge God.' So then, each of us will give an account of ourselves to God. Therefore, let us stop passing judgment on one another. Instead, make up your mind not to put any stumbling block or obstacle in the way of a brother or sister. Let us therefore make every effort to do what leads to peace and to mutual edification."*

The important thing is that we should not judge or argue, whether you celebrate Christmas or not. We are still children of God, heading toward heaven.

What Matters Most Is That Jesus Is Born Anew in Our Hearts

As we celebrate Christmas, let us allow Jesus Christ to be born anew within us. Let us change our character, speech, dress, and behavior, becoming new creations in the eyes of God.

2 Corinthians 5:17: *"Therefore, if anyone is in Christ, the new creation has come: The old has gone, the new is here!"*

Salvation Is the True Meaning of Christmas

There is no meaning in celebrating Christmas if you are not saved. Give your life to Jesus, my friend, for the Word of God says:

Matthew 1:21:

"She will give birth to a son, and you are to give Him the name Jesus, because He will save His people from their sins."

God Bless Everyone Who Reads This Message of the Word.

Wishing You a Merry Christmas!

CHAPTER 02

WHERE DOES THE BIBLE SAY CHRISTIANS SHOULD CELEBRATE CHRISTMAS?

In the previous section of this lesson, we analyzed in depth about Christmas and explored six (6) main biblical reasons why Christians celebrate the Christmas holiday.

Where Does the Bible Say Christians Should Celebrate Christmas?

Have you ever asked yourself that question, or has anyone ever asked you the same? Perhaps you celebrate this holiday simply because you feel like it.

We celebrate Christmas for many reasons—too many to explain fully in this space.

However, today I want to conclude by sharing five key reasons that compel Christians around the world to celebrate Christmas. These reasons include:

(7) We Celebrate Christmas to Commemorate the Birth of Our Savior, Jesus Christ of Nazareth

The Bible says in **Luke 2:10-11:** *"But the angel said to them, 'Do not be afraid. I bring you good news that will cause great joy for all the people. Today in the town of David a Savior has been born to you; He is the Messiah, the Lord.'"*

Hallelujah!

As we noted earlier, commemorating the birth of Jesus Christ does not mean He was born on December 25, as there is no specific biblical evidence indicating His exact birthdate.

It's important to remember that we are not celebrating a date but the event of the Savior's birth. Some people, overwhelmed by life's challenges, mistakenly think Christmas is about celebrating a particular day or date. But that's not the case!

For those caught up in such confusion, Christmas has become a puzzle as they try to determine the exact day or date Jesus was born.

The day or date means nothing to us; it has no significance at all! What matters is commemorating the Lord's coming, and that is why we celebrate.

The Prophet Isaiah Foretold Jesus' Birth

Isaiah prophesied about the birth of Jesus approximately 700 years before His arrival, saying:

"...the virgin will conceive and give birth to a son, and will call him Immanuel." (Isaiah 7:14)

The prophecy of Prophet Isaiah is indeed true and certain. Many prophecies have been made, but Isaiah's prophecy has been fulfilled because the Lord has truly been born. The birth of Jesus Christ is a miracle that has never happened before and will never happen again, as His birth was through the power of the Holy Spirit.

Even at birth, Jesus was already clothed with power and might. Think about it—what kind of child is born with such divine authority? The Bible describes Him as being called a "man-child" at birth, not just a baby boy, indicating that He was already endowed with extraordinary strength. He is Immanuel, "God with us" (**Matthew 1:23**).

---

(8) We Celebrate to Remember the Coming of Salvation to Humanity

The Bible says in **Hebrews 2:3:** *"How shall we escape if we ignore so great a salvation? This salvation, which was first announced by the Lord, was confirmed to us by those who heard him."*

We all know that humanity was lost after Adam and Eve's fall into sin in the Garden of Eden. Humanity was considered unworthy of eternal life. But because God loved the world—that is, He loved you and me—He sent His only Son, Jesus Christ, so that whoever believes in Him may have eternal life (**John 3:16**).

In simple terms, we celebrate this day to remember the salvation brought by Jesus Christ, for in Him lies true eternal life.

John 1:4: *"In Him was life, and that life was the light of all mankind."*

(9) We Celebrate to Remember God's Victory through Jesus Christ Over the Evil Powers of Satan Under the Sun

LISTEN:

The Bible says: *"But when the set time had fully come, God sent His Son, born of a woman, born under the law, to redeem those under the law, that we might receive adoption to sonship."* (**Galatians 4:4-5**)

Before the coming and acceptance of Jesus Christ, we were under the law, serving the gods of our ancestors. We were people without God in this world. Therefore, we could not become children of God—though we were His creation, we lacked divine sonship.

Seeing this, the Lord God sent His Son to be born under the law so that He might redeem us all and grant us the status of being children of God. God restored the fellowship of His Spirit with humanity, a relationship that had been lost in the Garden of Eden after the fall into sin.

John 1:12-13: *"Yet to all who did receive Him, to those who believed in His name, He gave the right to become children of God—children born not of natural descent, nor of human decision or a husband's will, but born of God."*

1 John 3:1-2: *"See what great love the Father has lavished on us, that we should be called children of God! And that is what we are! The reason the world does not know us is that it did not know Him. Dear friends, now we are children of God, and what we will be has not yet been made known. But we know that when Christ appears, we shall be like Him, for we shall see Him as He is."*

If the Lord Jesus had not been born, we would have remained under Satan's dominion, children of the devil forever.

But thanks be to God, because through the birth of Jesus Christ, we have received grace and love, becoming children of the living God.

---

(10) We Celebrate This Holiday to Remember the Coming of the Gospel to the World

The Bible says in **Mark 1:1:** *"The beginning of the gospel of Jesus Christ, the Son of God."*

Jesus Himself is the Gospel.

When He was born, the Gospel was born under the sun for the first time, for He is the Word. The Gospel is the Good

News that brings salvation, the Word of God offering salvation to everyone who believes. The Bible clearly states this:

Luke 2:10: *"But the angel said to them, 'Do not be afraid. I bring you good news that will cause great joy for all the people.'"*

The angel of the Lord declared that the coming of Jesus Christ into the world was the arrival of Good News bringing great joy. This means the Gospel had come, filled with joy that transforms the wicked and cruel into new, good, compassionate, and loving people.

Romans 1:16: *"For I am not ashamed of the gospel, because it is the power of God that brings salvation to everyone who believes: first to the Jew, then to the Gentile."*

---

(11) Through the Birth of Jesus Christ, We Have Received a Better Faith

Thus far, we have explored ten (10) foundational reasons for celebrating Christmas.

There are countless reasons why we Christians celebrate Christmas with great joy. The day of the Messiah's birth is a significant day, as it marks the remembrance of the arrival of Christianity in the world. The Bible speaks about this in **Hebrews 12:2:**

"Fixing our eyes on Jesus, the pioneer and perfecter of faith. For the joy set before Him, He endured the cross, scorning its shame, and sat down at the right hand of the throne of God."

2 Peter 1:1: *"Simon Peter, a servant and apostle of Jesus Christ, to those who through the righteousness of our God and Savior Jesus Christ have received a faith as precious as ours."*

The Christian faith we have received is the most precious faith, surpassing all other beliefs in the world. There is no greater honor or significance than being a Christian. A Christian is an essential figure on Earth, for they are God's representative and ambassador of His Kingdom in the world.

Therefore, if Jesus had not been born, this Christian faith—carrying grace, truth, blessings, mercy, power, authority, and the fullness of God's might—would not exist on Earth (**John 1:16-17; 1 Peter 5:10-12; Ephesians 1:3; 1 Corinthians 2:4-5; Matthew 16:18-19; Luke 10:17-19**).

But through the birth of Jesus Christ, we received the most excellent faith.

Note:

Let me share this secret with you — do you know that there would be no cross without the birth of Jesus Christ of Nazareth? The cross required Jesus to be born under sin, even though He never committed any sin (**Hebrews 4:15**).

Now listen carefully, my friend: this celebration has no true meaning for you if Jesus Christ has not been born within your heart. The real significance lies in Jesus being born in you. For Jesus to be born in you means surrendering your life to Him — it means being saved.

Romans 8:37: "Yet in all these things we are more than conquerors through Him who loved us."

1 Corinthians 15:57: "But thanks be to God, who gives us the victory through our Lord Jesus Christ."

Behold, we have no other path to victory except through Jesus Christ alone.

As we conclude celebrating all these memories, it is equivalent to celebrating victory over every aspect of our spiritual and even physical lives. When we are in the Lord Jesus, we are saved.

Let me tell you this — a saved person, on this very day of Christmas, sheds tears of joy because of the coming of our Lord Jesus, our Redeemer. They cannot fully explain everything they feel because spiritual matters are vast and beyond complete explanation (**Psalm 119:96**).

We have mentioned that there are many biblical reasons that make us celebrate this Christmas holiday.

But let it be remembered that spiritual matters are recognized by a spiritual person, while for a person of the flesh, on this day of the remembrance of the coming of the Lord Jesus, it is foolishness, and to them, it is quite normal and even a day to plan for rebellion. Remember, the wages of sin is death; but the gift of God is eternal life in Christ Jesus (Romans 6:23; John 10:9-10).

After death comes judgment, my brother (Hebrews 9:27).

Why don't you use this time to reflect on how your life stands before God? How long will you continue in your sins?

COME TO THE LORD JESUS CHRIST TODAY. The door of grace is still open for you. The Lord Jesus needs you to make Him the Lord and Savior of your life.

Shalom

CHAPTER 03

WHY IS CHRISTMAS ON DECEMBER 25?

Is December 25 mentioned in the Bible?

Let's begin by listening to Jesus as He refers to a passage connected to His mission:

Luke 4:18-21 (NIV): *"The Spirit of the Lord is on me, because he has anointed me to proclaim good news to the poor. He has sent me to proclaim freedom for the prisoners and recovery of sight for the blind, to set the oppressed free, to proclaim the year of the Lord's favor."*

Then he rolled up the scroll, gave it back to the attendant, and sat down. The eyes of everyone in the synagogue were fastened on him. He began by saying to them, "Today this scripture is fulfilled in your hearing."

In Luke 4:18, Jesus declares that He came to proclaim freedom for the prisoners. This is the mission Jesus came to fulfill—to set captives free.

Jesus fully understood that the specific date when prisoners were historically set free was December 25. This is why we celebrate His coming on that date.

Biblical Reference to December 25:

Jeremiah 52:29-32 (NIV): *"In the eighteenth year of Nebuchadnezzar's reign, he took 832 people from Jerusalem into exile. In the twenty-third year of Nebuchadnezzar's reign, Nebuzaradan, commander of the imperial guard, took 745 more Jews into exile—a total of 4,600 people."*

"In the thirty-seventh year of the exile of Jehoiachin king of Judah, on the twenty-fifth day of the twelfth month, Evil-Merodach king of Babylon, in the year he became king, released Jehoiachin king of Judah from prison. He spoke kindly to him and gave him a seat of honor higher than those of the other kings who were with him in Babylon."

On the twenty-fifth day of the twelfth month, King Jehoiachin of Judah was released from prison. This historical act of liberation mirrors the spiritual freedom Jesus came to offer humanity. Therefore, December 25 stands as a significant date symbolizing liberation and redemption through Jesus Christ.

What Did We Learn from Jeremiah 52:31?

We discovered that December 25 is the date when prisoners were set free. So, what did Jesus come to do on Earth?

Luke 4:18 (NIV): *"The Spirit of the Lord is on me, because he has anointed me to proclaim good news to the poor. He has sent me to proclaim freedom for the prisoners, and recovery of sight for the blind, to set the oppressed free."*

Isaiah 61:1 (NIV): *"The Spirit of the Sovereign Lord is on me, because the Lord has anointed me to proclaim good news to the poor. He has sent me to bind up the brokenhearted, to proclaim freedom for the captives and release from darkness for the prisoners."*

Introduction

The Spirit of the Lord is upon me today to preach good news to you, the humble, and to set the captives free. I declare freedom for the captives and release from the prisons of death, illness, and bondage. The time for your release has come.

You may have been freed long ago, yet remained unaware because no one ever told you. This message is an announcement of your freedom in Jesus' name.

When Jesus proclaimed freedom to those sitting in the synagogue, some rejected His message, saying, "We are not prisoners; we are Abraham's descendants."

Jesus responded, saying, *"If you were truly Abraham's children, you would not reject me."*

Similarly, there are people today who are spiritually bound yet deny it. They say, "I am not imprisoned, I am not sick, I am fine," because they lack understanding, just like those in Jesus' time.

Luke 4:16-21 (NIV)

"He went to Nazareth, where He had been brought up, and on the Sabbath day, He went into the synagogue, as was His custom. He stood up to read, and the scroll of the prophet Isaiah was handed to Him. Unrolling it, He found the place where it is written: 'The Spirit of the Lord is on me, because He has anointed me to proclaim good news to the poor. He has sent me to proclaim freedom for the prisoners and recovery of sight for the blind, to set the oppressed free, to proclaim the year of the Lord's favor.' Then He rolled up the scroll, gave it back to the attendant, and sat down. The eyes of everyone in the synagogue were fastened on Him. He began by saying to them, 'Today this scripture is fulfilled in your hearing.'"

Spiritual Captivity and Freedom

Many people have been taken captive, trapped in pits, and held by an enemy determined not to release them. That is why Jesus came—to proclaim their freedom and let them know that their release is already granted. You may have been bound, but the chains were loosened without your knowledge. You may have been healed but still see yourself as sick because no one announced your freedom.

Who Spoke These Words? The one who declared this prophecy was the prophet Isaiah. He referred to the one who binds people and holds them captive, refusing to set them free. The one who binds people is Satan.

Isaiah 14:12-17 (NIV)

"How you have fallen from heaven, morning star, son of the dawn! You have been cast down to the earth, you who once laid low the nations! You said in your heart, 'I will ascend to the heavens; I will raise my throne above the stars of God; I will sit enthroned on the mount of assembly, on the utmost heights of Mount Zaphon. I will ascend above the tops of the clouds; I will make myself like the Most High.' But you are brought down to the realm of the dead, to the depths of the pit. Those who see you stare at you, they ponder your fate: 'Is this the man who shook the earth and made kingdoms tremble, the man who made the world a wilderness, who overthrew its cities and would not let his captives go free?'"

Spiritual Prisons

In earthly terms, when people break the law, they are imprisoned according to the severity of their crimes—some for days, months, or years, and others for life. However, Satan imprisons people for life. That's why Jesus came—to free those held captive by Satan and proclaim their freedom.

These prisons are not physical but spiritual. You may be physically fine, but your work may be bound. You may have a good job but be imprisoned by sickness. You may have once seen clearly, but now your spiritual eyes are blinded.

Today, the Lord has come to set you free, restore you, and help you see opportunities, breakthroughs, and blessings in Jesus' name.

The One Who Holds People Captive

The one who holds people captive neither likes nor intends to set them free. His job is to bind and imprison. However, when he sees someone coming to set captives free, he becomes very aggressive. He hates seeing anyone released from prison and causes problems to prevent their freedom. He is ruthless and determined that no one should be freed or return to their rightful place.

Where Is "Home"?

You might have once had a happy marriage, but suddenly, peace turned into constant conflict. Every day becomes a fight between you and your spouse. Even asking for something small like a toothbrush results in arguments. But today, the Lord wants to restore your joy in Jesus' name.

Freedom from Indecision

Jesus sent His disciples to the city gate at a crossroads to free two donkeys—a mother and her colt. They were tied, unable to move forward into work, business, or marriage.

They were stuck at a crossroads, unable to make decisions. You might also be bound at a crossroads, unable to decide or move forward. Today, the Lord has come to set you free so that you can make decisions, start your work, launch your business, and move forward.

Matthew 21:1-2 (NIV) *"As they approached Jerusalem and came to Bethphage on the Mount of Olives, Jesus sent two disciples, saying to them, 'Go to the village ahead of you, and at once you will find a donkey tied there, with her colt by her. Untie them and bring them to me.'"*

Hidden Spiritual Bondage

Witches and spiritual oppressors who bind people often stay closer to their victims than the clothes they wear. The person binding you could be a neighbor, friend, or even a family member. They might appear to be helping you, perhaps even paying for your education, but their assistance could be a trap. The same person helping you might be the one holding you captive, keeping you stuck at a crossroads where you can't decide whether to build a house, start a business, or pursue a career.

God's Authority Over Captivity

Jesus instructed His disciples that if anyone questioned why they were untying the donkeys, they should answer, *"The Lord has need of them."*

Those who have bound you don't want to see you succeed. When they see your business growing or your progress increasing, they become furious, trying to block and hinder your success. But the Lord has come to set you free because He has a purpose for your life.

Matthew 21:3 *"If anyone says anything to you, say, 'The Lord needs them,' and they will send them right away."*

Spiritual Bondage and Freedom

There is someone out there who is spiritually bound. Every time they get a job, they are dismissed. Someone else might be attending church, but their spirit is tied to someone else's business or property. That person benefits from their labor while they continue to sink into hardship. Finding food has become a struggle. They remain jobless, stuck in the same place. The captor doesn't want them to escape and has assigned spiritual guards to ensure they stay imprisoned— just as physical prisoners are guarded by wardens.

Spiritual Oppression in Real Life

I read a story recently about a pastor who killed his wife, a university professor. Don't assume it was simply due to stress or the wife's faults. This is the work of a spiritual prison warden guarding and manipulating lives until tragedy strikes.

Jesus mentioned prisoners tied at the crossroads. Though their captors were nearby, Jesus instructed His disciples to say, *"The Lord needs them."*

Bound Lives and Broken Dreams

Maybe your marriage is on the verge of collapse, and you can't seem to make decisions. Consider this example: Prisoners may want to wear suits and ties, but once imprisoned, they are forced to wear yellow uniforms and shorts. They eat only what is provided to them.

You might think, *"I'm not bound,"* but remember, worldly dignity comes from three things: what you eat, what you wear, and where you live. You might long to drive a car to work, but you are bound and forced to walk on foot.

Satan wasn't inside Joshua the High Priest; he stood outside to resist him. Similarly, God wants you to reclaim your destiny, enter your kingdom, and possess your inheritance. Maybe you once owned a successful business, but now you buy from others because you have been spiritually restrained.

Manipulated Lives and Stolen Dreams

Perhaps you used to sleep well, but witches know that if you rest, you will commune with God. Now, when you lie down at 9 p.m., you suddenly can't sleep. When it's time to rise early for work, sleep returns heavily. Your physical state has been manipulated to keep you jobless and ineffective.

Acceptance of Bondage

Some people remain imprisoned for so long that they become accustomed to it. You hear them say, *"My sickness has returned,"* or *"My high blood pressure is acting up again."*

When the Israelites were leaving Egypt, Pharaoh devised strategies to keep them enslaved. They ate bread and fine meals, and when they were freed, they longed to return to Egypt despite the slavery.

Similarly, Satan can keep you imprisoned long enough that you begin to accept and even enjoy your captivity. He creates conditions that make you comfortable in spiritual bondage, causing you to settle in captivity without realizing it.

Spiritual Bondage and Deliverance

A person can be bound, making every effort seem impossible. You might be a servant of the Lord but still struggle with immorality or gossip, showing signs of spiritual captivity. The forces of darkness do not willingly release people from their prisons. The world cannot set you free, and Satan is not your friend; he is your enemy, crafting plans to keep you in bondage.

Someone bound in a spiritual pit often shows a hardened heart and a corrupted character. You might notice someone's eyes deteriorating, needing new glasses monthly. I once prayed for a young woman who came to church wearing glasses, and she was completely healed. At times, you may see someone suffering from leg pain—after prayer, they are told to rise and walk, yet they remain afflicted because their captor refuses to let them go.

God's Call for Freedom

The Lord declares:

"I, the Lord, have called you in righteousness; I will take hold of your hand. I will keep you and will make you to be a covenant for the people and a light for the nations, to open the eyes of the blind, to free captives from prison, and to release those who sit in darkness." — **Isaiah 42:7**

When imprisoned, you are blind to what is happening in the outside world. You cannot see progress, whether your descendants are thriving or failing. The first tactic of spiritual captivity is to cause blindness. A spiritually blind person rejects invitations to church or dismisses calls to repent from sin, viewing them as a joke because they cannot see the truth—they are spiritually captive.

Mental and Spiritual Confusion

When someone is mentally or spiritually imprisoned, their mind stops functioning properly. Their vision becomes clouded. You might find someone living in a trash heap, yet when told to leave, they reply, *"I'm living in America, enjoying life. Stop bothering me."* This isn't the person speaking but the evil spirits holding them captive.

Surprisingly, many who spread harmful messages may appear well-dressed to lure others into sin. You might wonder why someone would meet a stranger at a hotel and commit adultery—it isn't their rational mind at work but a result of spiritual blindness.

Humility Toward God's Word

A Christian must receive God's Word with humility. If you find yourself stuck in life, it might be because you haven't humbled yourself before God's Word. When God's Word is spoken, you must grasp it, apply it, and let it guide you to your destiny.

Do you humble yourself before the Word of God? Preachers aren't here to entertain but to deliver life-changing messages. Hold onto every Word from their mouths and apply it to your life.

Moses conveyed many words from God, and Jethro responded, *"All that you have spoken we will do."* The Bible says that anyone who hears God's Word but does not act on it is like someone looking at themselves in a mirror and immediately forgetting their appearance. However, the one who listens and obeys is like a wise person who built their house on a rock. When floods and winds come, they will stand firm.

May the Lord Establish You

May the Lord establish you again, enabling you to build your house on the rock, in Jesus' name.

Spiritual Blindness and Deliverance

There are blind professors, businesspeople, and ministers—people stuck in limited situations. Some are trapped in small businesses with no progress, selling only snacks, flour, or chapatis, unable to expand their sources of income. A person's captivity begins with spiritual blindness. Once blind, they are placed in a spiritual prison. Someone spiritually blinded might think they are in a good place, unaware they are lost in a wilderness or forest. You might invite them to seek a job, but they refuse because they are imprisoned. Today, may the Lord awaken you from wherever you are spiritually asleep, in Jesus' name.

Dark Houses of Captivity

Dark spiritual houses are filled with people's destinies, stars, marriages, jobs, and wealth. If your life seems dark or you're uncertain about your future, it may be because you have been bound and placed in a dark house, blinded from seeing clearly.

The Lord's Proclamation of Freedom has already been declared. When you hear this proclamation, come out of every captivity—whether it's a job-related prison, a marital prison, or any spiritual bondage. It's time to break free! Don't wait for someone to come to you; when you hear the Proclamation, step out of captivity and into your destiny, in Jesus' name. May the Lord set you free today from wherever you've been held back by the enemy. I command the fire of God to release you, in Jesus' name!

Breaking Free Through Jesus

Satan once opposed Jesus when He proclaimed freedom to the captives. They dragged Him, intending to throw Him into a valley, but He passed right through them unharmed. This is your time to run into the house of the Lord and declare, "Whether You bless me or not, Lord, I will remain in Your presence." This is not the time to be jobless, stuck in a troubled marriage, or living in darkness. Today, pass through the forces blocking your path, in Jesus' name.

Refuse to Stay Stagnant

Don't accept your current state. If you start working, don't settle for mediocrity. If you're in a troubled marriage, don't remain in that suffering without seeking God's intervention. Refuse to remain stuck with a small business or limited income. When you marry, be fruitful. When you work, aim to build. When you start a business, expect success. When you hold a job, strive for growth. Witches and spiritual oppressors rejoice when you remain in hardship.

When the Israelites received the proclamation of freedom from slavery, they left Egypt with wealth and possessions. May the Lord set you free today, along with your job, business, education, and every part of your life, in Jesus' name!

Proclamation of Freedom and Deliverance

"To say to the captives, 'Come out,' and to those in darkness, 'Show yourselves.' They will feed along the roads and find pasture on every barren hill. They will neither hunger nor thirst, nor will the desert heat or the sun beat down on them. He who has compassion on them will guide them and lead them beside springs of water. I will turn all my mountains into roads, and my highways will be raised up." —Isaiah 49:9-11

A sorcerer may bind someone due to their sins, making the captivity seem justified. However, when someone stronger arises, they can set the captives free—even those legally bound by their transgressions. God declares that He will confront those who have bound others and command their release. Today, Jesus has come to seek and free those held captive because of their sins.

Breaking Spiritual Bondage

A person's spirit, body, or life can be captured and held. Someone might be spiritually restrained from studying, conceiving, or succeeding. But God comes to break every chain (Job 33:20-30). Jesus, our Mighty Savior, desires you to experience joy and peace once again. The Lord wants you to come out of dark pits and step into success and a joyful marriage, in Jesus' name.

The Lord's Power to Deliver

"This is what the Lord Almighty says: The people of Israel and the people of Judah are oppressed. All who took them captive hold them fast, refusing to let them go. But their Redeemer is strong; the Lord Almighty is His name. He will vigorously defend their cause so that He may give rest to the land but unrest to those who live in Babylon." — Jeremiah 50:33-34

When you hear this Proclamation, do not harden your heart. Run to the Lord's house and meet Jesus. If you receive Jesus as your Lord and Savior, He will set you, your family, and everything concerning you free.

Example of Deliverance

"In the thirty-seventh year of the exile of Jehoiachin king of Judah, in the twelfth month, on the twenty-fifth day of the month, Evil-Merodach king of Babylon, in the year he became king, released Jehoiachin king of Judah from prison. He spoke kindly to him and gave him a seat of honor higher than those of the other kings who were with him in Babylon." —Jeremiah 52:31-32

The Mission of Jesus

"The Spirit of the Lord is on me, because He has anointed me to proclaim good news to the poor. He has sent me to proclaim freedom for the prisoners and recovery of sight for the blind, to set the oppressed free." —Luke 4:18

Shalom.

CHAPTER 04

WHY DO CHRISTIANS USE THE CHRISTMAS TREE?

In this fourth chapter, we will learn why Christians use the Christmas tree by examining four key aspects:

1. **The History of the Christmas Tree.**
2. **Why Do Christians Use the Christmas Tree?**
3. **Two Things to Avoid During the Christmas Celebration.**
4. **Clarifications for Christmas Opponents.**

Key Verse to Remember: *"The glory of Lebanon will come to you—the juniper, the fir, and the cypress together—to adorn my sanctuary; and I will glorify the place for my feet."* —Isaiah 60:13

Introduction

During this season of celebrating Christmas, one of the most important decorative symbols associated with the holiday is the *Christmas tree*. This tree has become a worldwide symbol representing Christmas itself. Every year during this festive season, the Christmas tree is prominently displayed in churches and homes as a central decorative piece.

Interestingly, the Christmas tree has a historical background that predates the official introduction of the Christmas celebration.

However, due to false teachings, lack of biblical understanding, and misinterpretation of spiritual truths, some individuals have misrepresented the use of the Christmas tree. These critics often accuse Christians—especially those in Pentecostal churches—of engaging in pagan worship by using the Christmas tree, associating it with idols like Tammuz and pagan traditions.

The Truth Behind the Criticism

These accusations are baseless and stem from Satan's deceitful schemes aimed at distorting historical facts to divert Christians from their true faith. Therefore, it is essential to understand the historical context and interpret it correctly according to the standard of God's Word (the Bible).

By gaining proper biblical knowledge, we can differentiate between what is spiritually acceptable and what is not. This understanding helps Christians celebrate Christmas meaningfully while staying true to their faith.

Colossians 2:4-8: *"I tell you this so that no one may deceive you by fine-sounding arguments. For though I am absent from you in body, I am present with you in spirit and delight to see how disciplined you are and how firm your faith in Christ is. So then, just as you received Christ Jesus as Lord, continue to live your lives in Him, rooted and built up in Him, strengthened in the faith as you were taught, and overflowing with thankfulness. See to it that no one takes you captive through hollow and deceptive philosophy, which depends on human tradition and the elemental spiritual forces of this world rather than on Christ."*

Ephesians 4:14-15: *"Then we will no longer be infants, tossed back and forth by the waves, and blown here and there by every wind of teaching and by the cunning and craftiness of people in their deceitful scheming. Instead, speaking the truth in love, we will grow to become in every respect the mature body of Him who is the head, that is, Christ."*

Guarding Against False Teachings

There has been a great deal of misleading teaching using historical references related to the celebration of Christmas. The Word of God clearly warns us not to be deceived but to know the truth and hold firmly to it.

Note:
As Christians in the faith of salvation, our guiding light is not history but the Bible. The Bible is our compass and standard. Any historical information must be measured against the principles and teachings of the Word of God to determine its truth and relevance.

Even if a specific issue is not directly mentioned in Scripture, the Bible has provided principles for evaluating what is acceptable or unacceptable before God. *[2 Peter 1:19; Psalm 119:105; 2 Timothy 3:15-17]*

This is why we are here today—to study the Word of God accurately. Through this lesson, we will gain clarity and understanding of what is appropriate for us as saved Christians to follow.

1. History of the Christmas Tree

Origin of the Modern Christmas Tree

(Source: Christmas tree - Wikipedia)

The modern Christmas tree traces its origins to the Renaissance period in early modern Germany. It is believed that the tradition emerged in the 16th century, sometimes linked to the Protestant Christian reformer Martin Luther, who is said to have first added lit candles to an evergreen tree.

The earliest documented Christmas tree appears in a keystone sculpture of a private home in Turckheim, Alsace (then part of Germany, now France), dating back to 1576.

Though the Christmas tree is now a well-recognized holiday symbol, it was initially a pagan tradition unrelated to Christian celebrations. Some historians associate the early Christmas trees in Alsace around 1600 with pre-Christian customs.

According to *Encyclopedia Britannica*, ancient Egyptians, Chinese, and Hebrews used evergreen trees, wreaths, and garlands to symbolize eternal life. Tree worship was common among pagan Europeans and continued even after their conversion to Christianity. In Scandinavian traditions, homes and barns were decorated with evergreens at the New Year to ward off evil spirits, and trees were set up outside to feed birds during the winter.

During the Roman mid-winter festival *Saturnalia*, homes were adorned with wreaths made of evergreen plants—a practice that later influenced Christmas traditions.

The Vikings and Saxons also practiced tree worship, tying the evergreen to spiritual beliefs.

In Poland, an ancient pagan custom involved hanging a fir, spruce, or pine branch called *Podaniczka* from the ceiling. Alternatively, mistletoe was used. These branches were decorated with apples, nuts, cookies, colored paper, straw stars, ribbons, and colored wafers. Many believed the decorated branches possessed magical powers connected to harvest and success in the coming year.

By the late 18th and early 19th centuries, these pagan customs were almost entirely replaced by the German tradition of decorating a Christmas tree.

Analysis

As you've read above, before the advent of Christianity and the celebration of Christmas, pagan Europeans practiced rituals involving evergreen plants. They believed these trees possessed magical powers to ward off evil spirits, ensure good harvests, and bring prosperity in the coming year.

The evergreens were associated with the worship of gods like *Saturn*, the Roman god of agriculture, during festivals like *Saturnalia*. Even after the conversion of these pagans to Christianity, some of these customs persisted, merging with Christmas celebrations over time.

Is It Wrong for Christians to Use the Christmas Tree Since It Was Used by Pagans?

The answer is **no!**

Why?

It's essential to understand the Bible clearly. God's Word calls trees "the trees of the Lord." He is the Creator of all plants and trees.

Isaiah 41:19-20 states: *"I will plant in the wilderness the cedar, the acacia tree, the myrtle, and the olive tree; I will set in the desert the cypress tree, the pine, and the box tree together, that they may see and know, and consider and understand together, that the hand of the Lord has done this, and the Holy One of Israel has created it."*

Psalm 104:16 says: *"The trees of the Lord are full of sap, the cedars of Lebanon which He planted."*

As you can see, trees belong to God, not to pagans. Since trees are God's creation, it is not wrong for Christians to use them. It depends entirely on how we use them. Using any tree or plant as a means of glorifying God is perfectly acceptable.

Biblical Support for Using Trees to Glorify God

The Bible encourages using all creation to praise God:

"Praise Him, sun and moon; praise Him, all you shining stars. Praise Him, you highest heavens and you waters above the skies... Praise the Lord from the earth, you great sea creatures and all ocean depths... mountains and all hills, fruit trees and all cedars... Let them praise the name of the Lord, for He commanded, and they were created..." (Psalm 148:1-13).

"Your laws endure to this day, for all things serve You." (Psalm 119:91).

Thus, trees are among the many creations that should be used to glorify and praise the Lord in worship.

The Pagan Misuse of Trees

The mistake pagans made was not using trees but **misusing them.** In their ignorance, their biggest sin was **worshiping trees** and trusting them for protection instead of trusting the living God. They placed their faith in the trees rather than in God above.

God's Warning Against Idolatry

The Word of God warns us against having other gods and trusting in anything other than Him:

Habakkuk 2:18-20 says: *"What profit is the image, that its maker should carve it, the molded image, a teacher of lies, that the maker of its mold should trust in it, to make mute idols? Woe to him who says to wood, 'Awake!'; to silent stone, 'Arise!' Can it teach? Behold, it is overlaid with gold and silver, yet in it there is no breath at all. But the Lord is in His holy temple. Let all the earth keep silence before Him."*

Deuteronomy 16:21-22 states: *"You shall not plant for yourself any tree as a wooden image near the altar which you build for the Lord your God. You shall not set up a sacred pillar, which the Lord your God hates."*

See also **Exodus 20:3**, **Isaiah 44:14-19**, and **Psalm 52:7-8**.

Conclusion

As saved Christians, when we use Christmas trees, we do not use them with the same intentions as the pagans once did. Our meaning and purpose in using trees differ entirely from the pagan practices. **We neither exalt nor worship the tree**, and our faith does not rest on the tree but on **the Lord.**

Why Do Christians Use the Christmas Tree?

There are two main reasons:

1. As a Decorative Ornament for Celebration

Christians use the Christmas tree primarily as a festive decoration. During the Christmas season, you'll often see Christmas trees decorating church altars, doorways, and other parts of God's house.

This practice of decorating with trees is also supported by the Bible. Consider what God's Word says:

Isaiah 60:13: *"The glory of Lebanon shall come to you, the cypress, the pine, and the box tree together, to beautify the place of My sanctuary; and I will make the place of My feet glorious."*

Even inside **Solomon's Temple**, which he built for God, specific trees were used as decorations to beautify the holy place.
(See **2 Chronicles 3:5-6** and **1 Kings 6:14-18**).

2. Biblical Support for Using Trees During Festivals

Using trees for celebration is also biblically supported and not considered paganism. Look at what God's Word says in **Leviticus 23:39-41:**

"On the fifteenth day of the seventh month, when you have gathered in the fruit of the land, you shall keep the feast of the Lord for seven days; on the first day there shall be a sabbath-rest, and on the eighth day a sabbath-rest. And you shall take for yourselves the fruit of beautiful trees, branches of palm trees, the boughs of leafy trees, and willows of the brook; and you shall rejoice before the Lord your God for seven days. You shall keep it as a feast to the Lord for seven days in the year. It shall be a statute forever in your generations; you shall celebrate it in the seventh month."

Conclusion

For those questioning the biblical legitimacy of Christians using trees during festive seasons, the Scripture above provides clear support. If someone calls Christians "pagans" for using trees, they are simply **ignorant** of the Bible. God Himself **instituted the use of trees** during festivals, making it a **God-ordained practice** when used with the right intent.

A Symbol of the Tree of Life Through Jesus Christ the Savior

Why is the Christmas tree associated with the birth of Jesus? This connection is primarily a spiritual revelation. It may not be understood by someone thinking only in a physical sense.

Here's the explanation: After humanity fell into sin in the Garden of Eden, mankind was sentenced to death and banished from the Garden. Humanity was no longer allowed to eat from the Tree of Life, which God said would enable them to live forever. The Bible says that God guarded the way to the Tree of Life to prevent access (Genesis 3:22-24).

Sin is what separated us from the Tree of Life, bringing eternal death. We lost our way to the Tree of Life.

Jesus Christ was born into the world to save sinners and restore what was lost (Matthew 1:21; Luke 19:9-10).

When Jesus Christ was born, He became the way to the Tree of Life (John 14:6; Proverbs 3:18).

This is why the Christmas tree is often decorated with ornaments resembling fruits and shining stars or lights. The star or lights at the top of the tree symbolize Jesus Christ Himself (Matthew 2:1-11; Revelation 22:16; John 8:12). Remember, Jesus Christ is "the way." Decorating the tree with a star or light signifies that Jesus is the way to the Tree of Life.

The Spiritual Meaning of the Christmas Tree

The Christmas tree teaches two important truths:

1. **Jesus Christ Came to Restore Us to the Tree of Life.**
2. **Believers in Christ, Those Who Are Saved, Have the Right to Eternal Life**—to eat from the fruit of the Tree of Life. Hallelujah!

Revelation 22:1-5, 14: *"Blessed are those who wash their robes, that they may have the right to the Tree of Life and may enter the city by the gates."*

Revelation 2:7: *"Whoever has ears, let them hear what the Spirit says to the churches. To the one who is victorious, I will give the right to eat from the Tree of Life, which is in the paradise of God."*

This is why the Christmas tree has become a significant symbol around the world, representing Christmas. It explains why Christians continue using it in churches, homes, and other places during the festive season.

Shalom!

PART II

JESUS IS THE MANIFESTATION OF THE INVISIBLE GOD

CHAPTER 05

____

WHO IS JESUS?

As a human being, Jesus Christ was assumed into the Hypostatic union, which is the union of the divine and human natures in one Person. In this union, the Person of Christ was anointed, which means that he was chosen and equipped for a specific role or office.

Jesus Christ was anointed by God to be the savior of humanity. This anointing was part of God's plan for the redemption of the world, and it was fulfilled through the incarnation of Jesus Christ.

Therefore, we may fitly say that the Person of Christ was anointed, so far as the call to office was concerned, meaning that he was specifically chosen and equipped for his role as the savior of humanity.

While the Person of Christ was anointed for his office, it is his humanity that receives the actual supplies of

God's gifts, graces, and endowments necessary to fulfill that office.

The Holy Spirit plays a role in the anointing of Jesus Christ, but this role is subordinate to the will of the Son. The Holy Spirit executes the will of the Son as it pertains to the anointing of Jesus Christ with the Spirit.

The anointing of Jesus Christ occurred in three successive grades or stages. The first grade was at the incarnation, which is when Jesus was born and took on human form. This was the beginning of his anointing process, as he was united with humanity and began to receive the necessary supplies of God's gifts and graces.

The above passage emphasizes the importance of both the divine and human natures of Jesus Christ in the anointing process and the role of the Holy Spirit in executing the will of the Son in this process.

The second grade coincided with his baptism, which is when Jesus was publicly declared as the Son of God and began his ministry. This event marked a significant point in his anointing process, as he received further supplies of God's gifts and graces to fulfill his ministry.

The third and highest grade of Jesus' anointing was at his ascension, which is when he returned to heaven and sat down on his mediatorial throne. At this point, he received from the Father the gift of the Holy Spirit, which he would then bestow upon his Church in abundant measure.

This passage highlights the progressive nature of Jesus' anointing, which occurred in three successive stages. The highest stage was reached at his ascension, where he received the gift of the Holy Spirit from the Father to bestow upon his Church. This gift of the Spirit is seen as a crucial aspect of the Christian faith, empowering believers to live a life of faithfulness and service to God.

The Spirit in the Incarnation and Baptism of Christ

The first stage of the anointing of Jesus Christ occurred in His mother's womb before his birth and continued throughout his childhood and up to the age of 30. During this time, his humanity was endowed with all spiritual graces, and he was illuminated, guided, and preserved by the immediate operations of the Holy Spirit, who is the Third Person in the Godhead.

This early anointing of Jesus Christ was crucial in preparing him for his ministry, as it equipped him with the necessary spiritual gifts and graces to fulfill his role as the savior of humanity. It also ensured that he was guided and preserved by the Holy Spirit, who was working within him to prepare him for his mission.

The above passage highlights the importance of the early anointing of Jesus Christ, which occurred before his public ministry began. It emphasizes the role of the Holy Spirit in this process and highlights how this anointing prepared Jesus for his ultimate mission to save humanity.

The Holy Spirit has existed eternally as a member of the Holy Trinity, along with God the Father and God the Son. Genesis 1:1-2, confirms the existence of the Holy Spirit at the very beginning of creation, where the Spirit of God moved upon the face of the waters.

It is also important to note that throughout the Old Testament, there are many references to the Holy Spirit, including the prophecies of the coming of the Messiah and the work of the Spirit in empowering the prophets and leaders of Israel. The coming of the Holy Spirit at Pentecost, after Jesus' ascension, was a unique and powerful event, but it did not mark the beginning of the Spirit's existence or work in the world.

To neglect the existence of or minimize the power of the Holy Spirit is to do an injustice to the Christian Faith. Many churches lack the power and authority to complete their Christian work because they neither thoroughly comprehend nor properly emphasize the structure and power of the Holy Trinity.

We come now to succinctly consider Jesus's second anointing when He was formally consecrated unto His public mission and divinely endowed for His official work.

Matthew 3:16-17 describes a unique and significant event in the life of Jesus Christ. This passage describes the baptism of Jesus by John the Baptist, and the subsequent descent of the Holy Spirit upon him in the form of a dove. It also includes the voice of God the Father declaring Jesus as His beloved Son.

This event marks the beginning of Jesus' public ministry and is significant for several reasons. First, it is a clear demonstration of Jesus' willingness to identify with humanity and to submit himself to God's will. Second, it serves as a public declaration of Jesus' divine identity and authority, as affirmed by the voice of God the Father. Finally, it is a powerful testimony to the work of the Holy Spirit in empowering Jesus for his ministry.

Jesus Christ is the only absolute sinless, spotless, and sufficient sacrifice for the sins of the entire world, past, present, and future. This is a central tenet of the Christian faith and is affirmed throughout the New Testament. Jesus' sacrificial death on the cross is understood as the ultimate expression of God's love for humanity and how we can be reconciled to Him.

The baptism of Jesus described in Matthew 3:16-17 is a significant event in the life of Christ and serves as a powerful testimony to the work of the Holy Spirit and Jesus' divine identity and authority. It is also a reminder of the central importance of Jesus' sacrificial death on the cross for the forgiveness of our sins.

Luke 4:14 records that Jesus returned from the Jordan River "full of the Holy Spirit" and was led by the Spirit into the wilderness. This event marks the beginning of Jesus' public ministry, and it is significant for several reasons.

First, it affirms that Jesus' humanity was confirmed by the Holy Spirit. This demonstrates that Jesus was not only fully divine but also fully human and that he relied on the power of the Holy Spirit to carry out his ministry on earth.

Second, it underscores the importance of spiritual preparation and dependence on the Holy Spirit in ministry. Jesus' time in the wilderness was a period of testing and temptation, and it was only by the power of the Holy Spirit that he was able to resist the devil's schemes.

Finally, this event set the stage for the rest of Jesus' ministry, which was characterized by the power and presence of the Holy Spirit. Throughout the Gospels, we see Jesus performing miracles, healing the sick, and preaching the good news of the Kingdom of God, all by the power of the Holy Spirit.

Luke 4:14 highlights the importance of the Holy Spirit in Jesus' ministry and underscores the crucial role of spiritual preparation and dependence on the Spirit in carrying out God's work.

Luke 4:18-19, 21 is known as Jesus' "Nazareth manifesto" and it reveals the purpose and mission of His ministry on earth. Jesus was anointed by the Holy Spirit to preach the Gospel, to heal the broken-hearted, to bring freedom to those who were captive, to restore sight to the blind, and to set free those who were oppressed. This was the fulfillment of the prophecy from Isaiah 61 that Jesus read in the synagogue. Jesus' declaration that the Scripture was fulfilled in their hearing was a bold claim that He was the promised Messiah who had come to bring salvation and redemption to His people.

Isaiah 61 was seen by the Jews as a Messianic prophecy, and Jesus was essentially declaring Himself as the fulfillment of that prophecy. He was anointed by the Holy Spirit for the specific purpose of carrying out His ministry on earth - preaching the Gospel, healing the sick, delivering the oppressed, and ultimately offering Himself as the perfect sacrifice for the sins of humanity.

The fact that Jesus claimed this prophecy as being fulfilled in Himself was a significant moment in His ministry and caused a great stir among the people. It demonstrated His authority and divine mission and set the tone for the rest of His time on earth.

The first grade of Christ's unction from the Spirit was at the incarnation when His humanity was formed and endowed with perfect wisdom and faultless holiness. This was necessary because, as the Bible says, "all have sinned and fall short of the glory of God" (Romans 3:23), but Jesus was to be the sinless sacrifice for the sins of the world. Through the power of the Holy Spirit, Jesus was able to live a perfect and holy life, fulfilling the law and accomplishing the will of the Father.

The dual "anointing" of Jesus Christ was necessary for His unique role as the God-Man and the Mediator between God and humanity. The first anointing endowed

His humanity with all spiritual graces and faultless holiness from the moment of conception, while the second anointing bestowed upon Him the necessary supernatural powers and ministerial gifts for His public ministry. Both anointings were necessary for Jesus to fulfill His mission and demonstrate His perfect obedience to the Father.

Isaiah 11:2-3 is a prophetic passage that speaks of the coming Messiah who will be anointed by the Spirit of the Lord with wisdom, understanding, counsel, might, knowledge, and fear of the Lord. These characteristics are fulfilled in Jesus Christ, who is the Son of God and the promised Messiah. The anointing of the Holy Spirit upon Jesus was a confirmation of His divine mission and authority, and it empowered Him to carry out the work of God on earth.

"For He whom God hath sent speaketh the words of God; for God giveth not the Spirit by measure unto Him" (John 3:34). This at once brings out the pre-eminence of Christ, for He receives the Spirit as no mere man could. Observe the contrast pointed out by Ephesians 4:7, "But unto every one of us is given grace according to the measure of the gift of Christ." In none but the Mediator did "all the fullness of the Godhead" dwell "bodily" (Colossians 2:9). The uniqueness of the Spirit's relation to our Lord comes out again in Romans 8:2, "For the law of the Spirit of life in Christ Jesus hath made me free from the law of sin and death." Note carefully the words we have italicized: not only does this statement reveal to us the source of all Christ's actions, but it also intimates that more habitual grace dwells in Him than in all created beings.

The Holy Spirit in the ascension of Christ Jesus

"Therefore, being by the right hand of God exalted, and having received of the Father the promise of the Holy

Spirit, He hath shed forth this, which ye now see and hear" (Acts 2:33). This verse refers to the outpouring of the Holy Spirit on the day of Pentecost, which occurred after Christ's ascension to heaven. As stated in the verse, Jesus had been exalted to the right hand of God and had received the promise of the Holy Spirit from the Father. He then poured out the Spirit on His disciples, empowering them to preach the Gospel and perform miraculous works. This event marked the fulfillment of the third and highest degree of Christ's unction, which was bestowed on Him at His ascension.

This supreme ride of unction, when Christ was "anointed with the oil of gladness above his fellows" (Psalms 45:7) and which became apparent at Pentecost, was an ascension gift. The declaration which Peter gave of it was but a paraphrase of Psalm 68:18, "Thou hast ascended on high, Thou hast led captivity captive: Thou hast received gifts for men; yea, for the rebellious also, that the LORD might dwell among them."

That bountiful supply of the Spirit was designed for the erecting and equipping of the New Testament church "The Six Dispensation", and it was fitly bestowed after the ascension upon those for whom the Spirit was purchased. In this dispensation, the Holy Spirit indwells believers as the Comforter as impeccably Exhibited in John 14:16-26. This dispensation has lasted for almost 2,000 years, and no one knows when it will end. We do know that it will end with the Rapture of all born-again believers from the earth to go to heaven with Christ. Following the Rapture will be the judgments of God lasting for seven years.

Christ Bestows the Holy Spirit

Our Savior, Lord Jesus was anointed with the Holy Spirit for the execution of all His earthly ministries, and the performance of all His mediatorial work. His right to send the Spirit into the hearts of fallen human beings was acquired by His atonement.

Jesus was anointed with the Holy Spirit for the execution of His earthly ministries and mediatorial work is a central tenet of Christianity. Jesus is the Son of God and His mission on earth was to redeem humanity from sin and reconcile them with God.

The Holy Spirit is the center of Christianity. The Holy Spirit is the third person of the Trinity, along with God the Father and Jesus the Son. The Holy Spirit is the source of spiritual power and it works in the hearts of believers to transform their lives.

Jesus sent the Holy Spirit into the hearts of fallen human beings was acquired by His atonement, this reflects a particular interpretation of Christian doctrine. The idea is that through His death and resurrection, Jesus overcame the power of sin and death, making it possible for the Holy Spirit to enter into the hearts of believers and transform them from the inside out.

It was the well-earned reward of all His struggle and suffering. One of the paramount results of the impeccable satisfaction which Christ offered to God on behalf of His people, was His right now to bestow the Spirit upon them. Of old it was promised Him, "By His knowledge shall My righteous Servant justify many, for He shall bear their iniquities: therefore, will I divide Him a portion with the great, and He shall divide the spoil with the strong; because He hath poured out His soul unto death" (Isaiah 53:11, 12). According to the prophecy, the Messiah would justify many through His knowledge, meaning that He would make them righteous before God. This justification would come at a great cost, as the Messiah would bear the iniquities of those

He was justifying. This is a reference to the fact that Jesus Christ, the ultimate fulfillment of this prophecy, would bear the sins of humanity on the cross, taking upon Himself the punishment that we deserved.

The passage goes on to say that because the Messiah had poured out His soul unto death, He would be rewarded with a portion among the great and the spoil among the strong. This is a reference to the fact that Jesus' death and resurrection would ultimately result in His exaltation and victory over sin and death. Through His sacrifice, Jesus would conquer death and make a way for all who believe in Him to have eternal life.

This prophecy is a powerful reminder of the depth of God's love for humanity and the lengths to which He was willing to go to save us from our sins. It also serves as a reminder of the incredible sacrifice that Jesus made on our behalf and the magnitude of the gift of salvation that He offers to all who believe in Him.

So, too, His forerunner had announced, "He shall baptize you with the Holy Spirit and fire" (Matthew 3:11). This passage comes from the Gospel of Matthew and refers to the ministry of John the Baptist, who was baptizing people in the Jordan River as a sign of their repentance. John was preparing the way for Jesus, who would come after him and bring a new level of spiritual transformation to those who believed in Him.

When John said that Jesus would baptize people with the Holy Spirit and fire, he was speaking of a deeper level of spiritual renewal that would come through Jesus' ministry. The Holy Spirit is the third person of the Trinity and is often associated with spiritual transformation and renewal. The idea of being baptized with fire is a metaphor for the refining and purifying work of the Holy Spirit in the lives of believers.

In the New Testament, we see the fulfillment of this prophecy when the Holy Spirit comes upon the early believers on the day of Pentecost (Acts 2:1-4). The Holy Spirit gave them the power to speak in different languages and proclaim the message of the gospel with boldness. This event marked the beginning of a new era of spiritual renewal and transformation, as the Holy Spirit empowered believers to live out their faith in a new and powerful way.

Today, the Holy Spirit continues to work in the lives of believers, empowering them to live out their faith and bear witness to the gospel message. When we receive the gift of salvation through faith in Jesus Christ, we also receive the gift of the Holy Spirit, who comes to live within us and guide us in our journey of faith.

A Conjunct Mission

The conjunct mission of Jesus and the Holy Spirit is the cooperative work of the Son and the Spirit in the plan of salvation for humanity. This mission involves the Son's work of redemption, which was accomplished through His death and resurrection, and the Spirit's work of revealing and applying this redemption to the hearts and lives of believers.

The Holy Spirit is sent by the Son to convict the world of sin, righteousness, and judgment (John 16:8-11), to guide believers into all truth (John 16:13), and to bear witness to the Son (John 15:26). The Spirit also empowers believers for ministry (Acts 1:8) and produces in them the fruit of the Spirit (Galatians 5:22-23).

The conjunct mission of Jesus and the Holy Spirit is an expression of the unity of the Trinity, in which the Father, Son, and Holy Spirit work together in perfect harmony to accomplish the purposes of God's redemptive plan. It is through the work of the Son and the Spirit that believers are saved, sanctified, and empowered to serve God in the world.

Exhibit: "Come ye near unto Me, hear ye this; I have not spoken in secret from the beginning: from the time that it was, there am I: and now the Lord God and his Spirit hath sent Me" (Isaiah 48:16).

Isaiah 48:16 is a prophetic statement in which the Lord Jesus affirms that He had always conspicuously addressed the Nation and that He had not spoken in secret from the beginning. He indicates that from the time of Moses, when He appeared in the burning bush and called Himself "I am that I am" (Exodus 3), He had been speaking to His people clearly and unmistakably.

This passage is significant because it shows that Jesus was speaking through the Spirit of prophecy, indicating His divine nature and his role as the Messiah. It also demonstrates that Jesus has been present throughout human history, from the beginning of time, and that He is intimately involved in the work of salvation.

Furthermore, the passage reveals the unity of the Trinity, as Jesus speaks of the Lord God and His Spirit sending Him. This highlights the divine relationship between the Father, Son, and Holy Spirit, and emphasizes the importance of the work of the Spirit in the mission of the Son.

Thus, the verses emphasize the continuity of God's plan of salvation throughout history, with Jesus playing a central role in its fulfillment. It also emphasizes the importance of listening to His message and coming near to Him to receive salvation and guidance.

"The Lord hath created a new thing in the earth: A woman shall compass a man" (Jeremiah 31:22). The verse from Jeremiah 31:22 is a prophetic statement that refers to a new thing that the Lord has created on the earth. It speaks of a woman who will "compass" a man, which could be interpreted in different ways depending on the context and the translation.

Some scholars believe that this passage may be referring to the virgin birth of Jesus Christ, in which a woman, Mary, gave birth to a man, Jesus, without the involvement of a human father. This miraculous event was indeed a new thing on earth, and it fulfilled many prophecies from the Old Testament.

Others interpret this passage more figuratively, seeing it as a metaphor for the relationship between God and His people. In this interpretation, the woman represents the people of God, who will surround and embrace the man, who represents Jesus Christ, as their Lord and Savior. This interpretation emphasizes the close relationship between God and His people and the importance of following Jesus as the path to salvation.

Hence, the verse from Jeremiah 31:22 is a prophetic statement that speaks to the importance of Jesus Christ in God's plan of salvation, and the new thing that He brought to the earth through His life, death, and resurrection.

The Virgin Mary, under the overshadowing power of the Highest (Luke 1:35 And the angel answered and said unto her, The Holy Ghost shall come upon thee, and the power of the Highest shall overshadow thee: therefore, also that holy thing which shall be born of thee shall be called the Son of God.) was to conceive and bring forth a Child, without the help or cooperation of man. This transcendent wonder Isaiah calls a "sign" (7:14); Jeremiah "a new thing in the earth"; the New Testament record of which is, "When as his mother Mary was espoused to Joseph before they came together, she was found with child of the Holy Spirit" (Mathew 1:18).

"And the Child grew, and waxed strong in spirit, filled with wisdom, and the grace of God was upon Him. And Jesus increased in wisdom and stature, and in favor with God and man" (Luke 2:40, 52). The verses from Luke 2:40 and 2:52 describe the growth and development of Jesus Christ as a child. They emphasize that Jesus grew strong in spirit, was filled with wisdom, and had the grace of God upon Him. As He grew up, He continued to increase in wisdom and stature and favor with God and man.

These verses highlight the human side of Jesus, showing that He experienced a normal process of growth and development. At the same time, they also emphasize His divine nature, as His growth was accompanied by spiritual strength, wisdom, and favor with God.

The phrase "waxed strong in spirit" suggests that Jesus developed a strong connection with God from a young age and that He was guided by the Holy Spirit throughout His life. The mention of wisdom also underscores the importance of Jesus' teachings, which were marked by profound insights and deep understanding.

The verses from Luke 2:40 and 2:52 also point to the importance of Jesus' relationships with both God and man. They suggest that Jesus was not only close to God but also had positive interactions with other people, earning their favor and respect.

These verses provide insight into the formative years of Jesus Christ, highlighting His spiritual strength, wisdom, and close relationship with God. They also point to the importance of human relationships, suggesting that

Jesus valued and cultivated positive interactions with others.

The Holy Spirit played a crucial role in the incarnation of Jesus Christ and continued to guide Him throughout His earthly life. the Holy Trinity - the Father, Son, and Holy Spirit - in the workings of the divine plan.

The Holy Spirit played a vital role in the conception of Jesus Christ. It was through the power of the Holy Spirit that Jesus was conceived in the womb of Mary, without the involvement of a human father. This miraculous event is known as the virgin birth, and it marked the beginning of Jesus' earthly life.

Throughout His life, Jesus was guided by the Holy Spirit, who empowered Him to perform miracles, teach with wisdom and authority, and ultimately fulfill His mission of redemption through His death and resurrection. The Holy Spirit continued to work in and through the followers of Jesus after His ascension, empowering them to spread the message of salvation to the world.

The Father, Son, and Holy Spirit are three distinct persons in one Godhead. They work together in perfect harmony, with the Holy Spirit proceeding from the Father and the Son, to accomplish the divine plan of salvation. "From birth to baptism, the Holy Spirit directed Jesus' mental and moral development and strengthened and kept Him through all the years of preparation and toil, (Luke 4:1 And Jesus being full of the Holy Ghost returned from Jordan, and was led by the Spirit into the wilderness). He was in the Carpenter as truly as in the Messiah, and the work at the bench was as perfect as the sacrifice on the Cross". At first sight, such assertion may seem to derogate from the personal honor of the Lord Jesus, but if we perceive that, according to the order of the Trinity, the Spirit exercises His power only to execute the will of the Father and the Son, then the seeming difficulty disappears. So far is the interposition of the Spirit's operations from interfering with the glory of the Son, it rather reveals Him the more conspicuously: that in the work of redemption, the activities of the Spirit are next to those of the Son.

CHAPTER 06

THE SPIRIT UNITING TO JESUS

The binary types of Union

Matthew 28:19 is a key passage in Christian theology regarding the doctrine of the Trinity. The statement affirms that a proper exegesis, or critical interpretation, of the verse reveals two important truths about the nature of God.

The first truth is that the singular form of "name" in the verse indicates that God is one and that His nature is singular. This emphasizes the concept of monotheism, the belief in one God, which is a central tenet of Judaism and Christianity.

The second truth, according to the statement, is that within the unity of this one, God is three distinct persons, namely the Father, the Son, and the Holy Spirit. The statement emphasizes that the original Greek text of the verse reinforces this concept by including three definite articles before each person of the Trinity. This highlights the idea that each person of the Trinity is distinct and has a unique role in the Godhead.

Together, these two truths confirm that the nature of God is complex and multifaceted, yet unified. The concept of the Trinity affirms that God is both one and three, a concept that has been the subject of much theological debate and discussion throughout Christian history.

Matthew 28:19 presents highlights the importance of both the unity and diversity of God's nature and the concept of the Trinity as a fundamental doctrine of Christian theology.

There are two types of union between Christ and His people, namely judicial and vital (or legal and spiritual).

The judicial or legal union refers to the union that was made by God the Father between Jesus Christ, the Redeemer, and believers when He was appointed their federal Head. This union is based on law, and it means that Jesus represented believers and was responsible for them. The benefits of His redemptive work on the cross, such as forgiveness of sins and reconciliation with God, are imputed to believers as a result of this union. This union can be illustrated by the concept of suretyship, where a surety becomes liable for the debt of another person, and the payment made by the surety is considered as the payment of the debtor, absolving the debtor from any obligation to the creditor.

The vital or spiritual union, on the other hand, refers to the union between Christ and believers on a spiritual level. This union is based on faith, and it is described in the New Testament as a union between Christ and His Church, where believers are joined to Christ as branches are joined to a vine (John 15:1-8). This union is characterized by the indwelling of the Holy Spirit in believers, which enables them to participate in the life of Christ and to bear fruit for God.

Both types of union are important aspects of the believer's relationship with Christ. The judicial union ensures that believers are legally justified before God, while the spiritual union enables them to experience the fullness of life in Christ.

In John 6:44-45, Jesus speaks of a special relationship between the Father, Himself, and those who come to Him. The Father draws people to Jesus, and those who come are those who have listened and learned from the Father. This indicates a close connection between the Father and those who come to Jesus, and it emphasizes the role of the Father in salvation. It also suggests that those who come to Jesus have been given to Him by the Father. This truth is further developed in John 17, where Jesus prays for His disciples and for all who believe in Him through their message. In this prayer, Jesus speaks of the unity between Himself and the Father, and the unity between Himself and His disciples. He asks that His disciples may be one, just as He and the Father are one, and that they may be brought to complete unity so that the world may know that the Father sent Him. This prayer emphasizes the close relationship between Christ and His people, and the role of the Father in bringing them together.

Admittedly, as Jesus said the spirit's work is somewhat mysterious. Yet it is very real and necessary to bring about new life in Christ.

John 3:5 Jesus answered, "I tell you the truth, no one can enter the kingdom of God unless he is born of water and the Spirit. 6 Flesh gives birth to flesh, but the Spirit gives birth to spirit. 7 You should not be surprised at my saying, 'You must be born again.' 8 The wind blows wherever it pleases. You hear its sound, but you cannot tell where it comes from or where it is going. So, it is with everyone born of the Spirit."

In this passage, Jesus is teaching Nicodemus about the necessity of spiritual rebirth for entering the kingdom of God. He emphasizes that this rebirth is not a physical birth, but a spiritual one that comes from being born of the water and the Spirit. This can be understood as a reference to baptism, which is a symbol of washing away the old life and being born again in the Spirit.

Jesus explains that human beings can only give birth to physical life, but it is the Holy Spirit who gives birth to spiritual life. He then goes on to say that this rebirth is necessary and not something to be surprised about. He uses the metaphor of the wind to illustrate that the work of the Holy Spirit is mysterious and unseen, just like the movement of the wind.

Jesus emphasizes the importance of spiritual rebirth and the role of the Holy Spirit in bringing about this new life in believers. It also highlights the mysterious and powerful nature of the Holy Spirit's work in the lives of believers.

Internal "Drawing"

The preaching of the Gospel, or the Good News, is a central part of the Christian faith and is considered by many to be the primary means by which people come to faith in Jesus Christ and are reconciled to God.

Romans 10:14 states, "How then will they call on him in whom they have not believed? And how are they to believe in him of whom they have never heard? And how are they to hear without someone preaching?" This verse emphasizes the importance of preaching and sharing the Gospel message with others.

Similarly, 1 Corinthians 1:21 says, "For since, in the wisdom of God, the world did not know God through wisdom, it pleased God through the folly of what we preach to save those who believe." Again, this emphasizes the importance of preaching the Gospel as a means of bringing people to faith in Christ.

2 Corinthians 5:20 further emphasizes this point by describing believers as ambassadors for Christ and calling on them to implore others to be reconciled to God. This is an important reminder that as followers of Christ, we have a responsibility to share the Gospel message with others and to invite them to come to faith in Christ.

"Thy people shall be willing in the day of Thy power" (Psalms 110:3). It is by ethical inducement—" with cords of a man" (Hosea 11:4)—that the Holy Spirit draws humans to Christ.

Psalms 110:3 states, "Your people will offer themselves freely on the day of your power, in holy garments; from the womb of the morning, the dew of your youth will be yours." This verse suggests that God's people will willingly come to Him on the day of His power.

Similarly, Hosea 11:4 speaks of God's "cords of human kindness" or "cords of love" which draw His people to Himself. This suggests that God draws people to Himself through a loving and ethical approach, rather than through coercion or force.

This is consistent with the teachings of the New Testament, which emphasize the role of the Holy Spirit in drawing people to Christ. In John 6:44, Jesus states, "No one can come to me unless the Father who sent me draws him." In John 16:8-11, Jesus explains that the Holy Spirit convicts the world of sin, righteousness, and judgment, leading people to repentance and faith in Christ.

The Bible teaches that God draws people to Himself through a loving and ethical approach, using the Holy Spirit to convict and lead people to faith in Christ. This is in keeping with God's character as a loving and merciful God who desires all people to come to a knowledge of the truth and be saved.

2 Thessalonians 1:11 states that God fulfills all the good pleasure of His goodness and the work of faith with power. This emphasizes that it is through God's power and goodness that faith can be exercised and good works can be accomplished.

Similarly, Isaiah 53:1 speaks of the importance of the "arm of the LORD" being revealed for people to believe His report. This suggests that it is through God's power and revelation that people can come to faith in Him and believe in His message.

These verses highlight the central role that God plays in the process of salvation and faith. It is through His power, goodness, and revelation that people can believe and exercise faith. This is consistent with other biblical teachings, such as Ephesians 2:8-9, which states that salvation is a gift from God that is received through faith, not by our works or efforts.

These verses emphasize the importance of relying on God and His power in the process of salvation and faith. It is only through His goodness and revelation that people can believe exercise faith and accomplish good works in His name.

Spiritual Union with Christ

The Bible teaches that spiritual union with Christ is influenced both by the external preaching of the Gospel and the internal "drawing" of the Father.

On one hand, Romans 10:17 teaches that "faith comes from hearing, and hearing through the word of Christ." This emphasizes the importance of the external preaching of the Gospel as a means of bringing people to faith in Christ and establishing a relationship with Him.

On the other hand, Jesus Himself taught that no one can come to Him unless the Father draws them (John 6:44). This suggests that there is an internal work of the Father in the hearts of people, which enables them to respond to the Gospel message and come into a relationship with Christ.

These two aspects of spiritual union with Christ work together in the process of salvation. The external preaching of the Gospel is how people hear the message of Christ and have the opportunity to respond to it in faith. But it is the internal work of the Father in drawing people to Himself that enables them to respond in faith and enter into a relationship with Christ.

The Bible teaches that spiritual union with Christ is influenced both by the external preaching of the Gospel and the internal work of the Father in drawing people to Himself. These two aspects work together to bring people to faith and establish a relationship with Christ.

Philippians 3:12 emphasizes the importance of a vital principle being communicated to us before any vital act of faith can be exercised. This vital principle is the indwelling of Christ by His Spirit in the believer, which enables the believer to have faith and enter into a relationship with Christ.

Romans 6:3-5 further explains this concept by highlighting the believer's identification with Christ in His death and resurrection through baptism. Through this identification, the believer is united with Christ and empowered to live a new life in Him.

The metaphor of the head and body in 1 Corinthians 12:12-27 also emphasizes the believer's union with Christ. Just as the head directs and sustains the body, Christ directs and sustains His believers through His Spirit. And just as the members of a body are interconnected and interdependent, believers are interconnected and interdependent with one another in Christ.

The Bible teaches that the believer's union with Christ is vital to their faith and Christian life. This union is made possible through the indwelling of Christ by His Spirit and is characterized by a close and interdependent relationship between Christ and His believers.

"He that is joined unto the Lord is one spirit" with Him (1 Corinthians 6:17). 1 Corinthians 6:17 teaches that the believer who is joined to the Lord is one spirit with Him. This emphasizes the close and intimate union that exists between Christ and His believers through the indwelling of His Spirit.

The same Spirit that is in Christ as the Head of the church is also in the members of His body, which creates a vital union between them. This union is characterized by a shared identity, purpose, and life in Christ.

This truth of the mystical body of Christ is further elaborated in 1 Corinthians 12:12-27, which uses the metaphor of a human body to describe the relationship between Christ and His believers. Just as a body has many members, each with its function, so too does the body of Christ have many members with different gifts and roles.

Through the indwelling of the Holy Spirit, believers are united with Christ and with one another in a spiritual and organic union. This union is characterized by a shared life, a shared purpose, and a shared destiny.

The biblical truth of the mystical body of Christ emphasizes the close and intimate union between Christ and His believers through the indwelling of His Spirit. This union is characterized by a shared identity, purpose, and life in Christ, and is a vital aspect of the believer's faith and Christian life.

"For by one Spirit are we all baptized into one body, whether we be Jews or Gentiles" (1 Corinthians 12:13)—what could be plainer than that? 1 Corinthians 12:13 emphasizes the role of the Holy Spirit in uniting believers into one body, regardless of their ethnicity or background.

The verse states that "by one Spirit are we all baptized into one body," indicating that it is through the work of the Holy Spirit that believers are united together in Christ. This baptism refers to the spiritual baptism into Christ's body, which occurs at the moment of salvation when a person places their faith in Jesus Christ.

This baptism into one body is significant because it emphasizes the unity of all believers in Christ. It does not matter whether a person is a Jew or a Gentile, slave or free, male or female, all are united together in Christ through the work of the Holy Spirit.

This concept of unity in Christ is further emphasized in other parts of the New Testament, such as Galatians 3:28, which states that "there is neither Jew nor Greek, there is neither bond nor free, there is neither male nor female: for ye are all one in Christ Jesus."

"Hereby know we that we dwell in Him, and He in us, because He hath given us of His Spirit" (1 John 4:13). Thus, Christ is unto His people a Head not only of government but also of influence. 1 John 4:13 emphasizes the role of the Holy Spirit in affirming our relationship with

God through Christ. The verse states that we know we dwell in God, and He in us because He has given us His Spirit.

The Holy Spirit is a gift from God, given to believers as a seal of their relationship with Christ (Ephesians 1:13-14). The Spirit testifies to our adoption as children of God (Romans 8:15-16) and empowers us to live a life pleasing to God (Galatians 5:22-23).

In this sense, Christ is not only a Head of government but also of influence. He exerts His influence on our lives through the indwelling of the Holy Spirit, who transforms us from within and empowers us to live a life that honors God.

This truth of Christ as a Head of influence is further elaborated in Ephesians 4:15-16, which describes Christ as the Head of the body, who nourishes and supports the growth of each member of the body. As believers, we are called to submit to Christ's influence in our lives, allowing Him to shape and transform us through the work of His Spirit.

"The Spirit of life in Christ Jesus hath made me free from the law of sin and death" (Romans 8:2). states that "the Spirit of life in Christ Jesus has made me free from the law of sin and death."

Through the work of the Holy Spirit, believers are set free from the power of sin and death and are united with Christ spiritually and intimately. This union is so close that it can be described as Christ living in us and us living in Him.

This concept of Christ living in us is further emphasized in Galatians 2:20, where the Apostle Paul states, "I have been crucified with Christ, and I no longer live, but Christ lives in me. The life I now live in the body,

I live by faith in the Son of God, who loved me and gave himself for me."

Overall, Romans 8:2 and other passages in the New Testament highlight the intimate and real connection between Christ and believers through the work of the Holy Spirit. This connection is so close that it can be described as Christ living in us and us living in Him, and it brings freedom from the power of sin and death.

Galatians 4:6 indicates that the Holy Spirit is sent into our hearts as a result of our adoption as sons of God. This suggests a unique and intimate relationship with God that is different from the mere influence of the Word.

Before a person becomes a child of God, the Holy Spirit works through the Word to convict them of sin and draw them to faith in Christ. However, it is through the adoption process that the believer is given the fullness of the Spirit and experiences a deeper level of relationship with God as a son or daughter.

As Romans 8:14-16 explains, "For those who are led by the Spirit of God are the children of God. The Spirit you received does not make you slaves so that you live in fear again; rather, the Spirit you received brought about your adoption to sonship. And by him, we cry, 'Abba, Father.' The Spirit himself testifies with our spirit that we are God's children."

So, while the Word of God is essential in bringing people to faith in Christ, the adoption process brings believers into a deeper and more intimate relationship with God as His children, with the Holy Spirit bearing witness to this reality in their hearts.

"But if the Spirit of Him that raised Jesus from the dead dwell in you, He that raised Christ from the dead shall also quicken your mortal bodies by His Spirit that dwelleth in you" (Romans 8:11).

Romans 8:11 emphasizes the role of the Holy Spirit as the bond of union between us and Christ. Because the same Spirit that raised Christ from the dead dwells in us, we can have confidence that we too will be raised from the dead to eternal life.

This is because the Holy Spirit is the source of our spiritual life and power, and it is through His indwelling that we are united with Christ and share in His resurrection. As Paul explains in Ephesians 1:19-20, the same power that raised Christ from the dead is at work in us who believe.

Moreover, as we are conformed to the image of Christ through the work of the Holy Spirit, we will also share in His sufferings and ultimately in His glory. This is because the Spirit enables us to live in obedience to God and to endure trials and tribulations with faith and perseverance.

The Holy Spirit is the source of our spiritual life, the bond of union between us and Christ, and the power by which we are raised to new life and conformed to His image.

The indwelling of the Holy Spirit in believers is how God takes up His abode in them. This indwelling is a real and personal relationship with the triune God, and it is a distinguishing feature of the New Testament era of salvation. The presence of the Holy Spirit in the believer is both a guarantee of future glory (Ephesians 1:13-14) and a source of power for Christian living (Galatians 5:16-25).

CHAPTER 07

JESUS IS THE ETERNAL WORD

1.1 Introduction

The concept of Jesus Christ as the Eternal Word is foundational to Christian theology and central to the understanding of His divinity. The Gospel of John begins with a profound statement that encapsulates this truth: "In the beginning was the Word, and the Word was with God, and the Word was God" (John 1:1). This verse, rich in theological depth, establishes the pre-existence of Jesus Christ, affirming that He is not merely a historical figure or a prophet but the eternal, divine Logos, the very expression of God's nature and will.

1.2 The Pre-existence of Christ

The idea that Jesus existed before His incarnation is a cornerstone of Christian belief. Unlike any other human being, Jesus did not come into existence at the moment of His birth. Instead, He existed eternally with God the Father. The term "Word" (Logos in Greek) used by John is significant because it conveys the concept of divine reason, order, and communication. In both Jewish and Greek thought, Logos represented something much greater than human language; it was the divine principle that governs the cosmos.

John's assertion that "the Word was with God" emphasizes the distinct personhood of Christ, coexisting with God the Father, yet maintaining unity with Him. This coexistence is not a mere proximity but an intimate, relational union within the Godhead. Furthermore, the statement "the Word was God" unequivocally declares the divinity of Jesus. He is not a lesser being or a created entity; He is fully God, sharing the same essence as the Father.

1.3 Biblical Evidence for the Eternal Word

The pre-existence of Jesus is attested to throughout the New Testament. In John 8:58, Jesus Himself declares, "Before Abraham was, I am." This statement not only asserts His existence before Abraham, a patriarch who lived centuries before Christ's earthly life, but it also echoes the divine name revealed to Moses in Exodus 3:14, "I AM WHO I AM." By using the phrase "I am," Jesus aligns Himself with the God of Israel, the eternal, self-existent One.

The Apostle Paul also affirms the pre-existence and divinity of Christ in his letters. In Colossians 1:16-17, Paul writes, "For by Him all things were created that are in heaven and that are on earth, visible and invisible, whether thrones or dominions or principalities or powers. All things were created through Him and for Him. And He is before all things, and in Him all things consist." Here, Paul portrays Jesus not only as pre-existent but as the agent of creation, sustaining the universe by His power.

Hebrews 1:2 further supports this by stating that God "has in these last days spoken to us by His Son, whom

He has appointed heir of all things, through whom also He made the worlds." Jesus is the one through whom God created everything, reinforcing His eternal nature and divine authority.

1.4 The Logos in Old Testament Revelation

Although the full revelation of the Logos is found in the New Testament, the concept is rooted in the Old Testament. Various passages hint at the presence of a divine person who acts on behalf of God and embodies His word. For example, in Proverbs 8:22-31, Wisdom is personified and described as being present with God before the creation of the world, participating in the creation process. While not a direct reference to Christ, early Christians saw this as a foreshadowing of the Logos.

Furthermore, the "Angel of the Lord" in the Old Testament often speaks as God, identifies with God, and yet is distinct from God (e.g., Genesis 16:7-13; Exodus 3:2-6). Early Christian theologians interpreted these appearances as pre-incarnate manifestations of Christ, the Logos.

1.5 The Incarnation: The Word Made Flesh

John 1:14 states, "And the Word became flesh and dwelt among us, and we beheld His glory, the glory as of the only begotten of the Father, full of grace and truth." The incarnation is the pivotal moment where the eternal Word entered human history. The divine Logos, who existed with God from the beginning, took on human nature and lived among us. This profound mystery—God becoming man—is central to the Christian faith.

The incarnation reveals the depths of God's love and the extent of His desire to redeem humanity. The eternal Word did not remain distant or detached from His creation; instead, He entered into the human experience, sharing in our sufferings, joys, and limitations, yet without sin. In doing so, He provided the perfect revelation of God and the means for our salvation.

1.6 Theological Implications of the Eternal Word

Understanding Jesus as the Eternal Word has significant theological implications. It affirms that Jesus is not merely a messenger or a moral teacher but God Himself, worthy of worship and obedience. His pre-existence and role in creation establish His authority over all things, including life and death.

Moreover, the eternal nature of Christ provides the basis for our hope in eternal life. As the one who is eternal, Jesus offers eternal life to those who believe in Him. He is the source of all life, both physical and spiritual, and through Him, we are united with the eternal God.

The doctrine of the Eternal Word also emphasizes the continuity of God's plan throughout history. The same Word who was with God in the beginning is the one who became flesh to redeem us. This underscores the consistency and faithfulness of God, who has worked through the ages to bring about His purposes.

1.7 Conclusion

The concept of Jesus as the Eternal Word is central to the Christian understanding of His divinity. From the opening verses of John's Gospel to the teachings of the apostles, the Bible consistently presents Jesus as the pre-existent, divine Logos, who was with God and was God. His incarnation as the Word made flesh is the ultimate expression of God's love and the definitive revelation of His nature.

As we reflect on the Eternal Word, we are drawn into a deeper appreciation of who Jesus is and what He has done for us. He is the Alpha and Omega, the beginning and the end, the one through whom all things were made and the one who sustains all things. In Him, we find the fullness of life and the assurance of eternal hope.

Jesus as the Son of God

2.1 Introduction

The title "Son of God" is one of the most profound and significant designations given to Jesus Christ in the New Testament. This title encapsulates both His unique relationship with God the Father and His divine nature. Understanding what it means for Jesus to be the Son of God is crucial for grasping the core of Christian doctrine and the identity of Jesus as the Messiah, the Savior of the world. In this chapter, we will explore the meaning and significance of this title, its biblical foundations, and its implications for faith and theology.

2.2 The Biblical Foundation of the Title

The title "Son of God" is rooted in both Old and New Testament scriptures. In the Old Testament, the term is occasionally used to describe Israel (Exodus 4:22-23), the Davidic king (2 Samuel 7:14), and even angels (Job 1:6). However, these usages were more metaphorical and did not imply a divine nature. The New Testament, however, reveals a much deeper and more profound understanding of this title when applied to Jesus.

In the New Testament, Jesus is explicitly referred to as the "Son of God" in multiple instances, highlighting His unique and unparalleled relationship with God the Father. One of the most notable affirmations comes at Jesus' baptism, where a voice from heaven declares, "This is my beloved Son, in whom I am well pleased" (Matthew 3:17). This divine proclamation not only identifies Jesus as the Son of God but also affirms His mission and divine approval.

Another significant moment occurs at the Transfiguration, where God's voice again affirms Jesus' sonship: "This is my beloved Son, in whom I am well pleased; hear Him!" (Matthew 17:5). These divine endorsements set Jesus apart from all others, marking Him as the unique, eternal Son of God.

2.3 The Sonship of Jesus: More Than a Title

The title "Son of God" does not merely indicate a filial relationship but also signifies Jesus' divine nature and authority. In the cultural and religious context of the time, calling someone the "Son of God" would be tantamount to equating them with God Himself. This is evident in the reaction of the Jewish leaders when Jesus claimed God as His Father: "Therefore the Jews sought all the more to kill Him, because He not only broke the Sabbath but also said that God was His Father, making Himself equal with God" (John 5:18).

Jesus' sonship is unique in several ways:

1. Eternal Sonship: Unlike any other figure referred to as a "son of God," Jesus' sonship is eternal. He was not adopted or created as a son but is eternally begotten of the Father. This is affirmed in John 1:18, where Jesus is described as "the only begotten Son, who is in the bosom of the Father." This eternal generation indicates that Jesus shares the same divine essence as the Father, making Him co-equal and co-eternal with God.

2. Divine Authority: As the Son of God, Jesus possesses divine authority over all creation. This authority is evident in His teachings, miracles, and, ultimately, His resurrection. In John 10:30, Jesus states, "I and My Father are one," emphasizing His unity with the Father in purpose and essence. This divine authority also means that Jesus has the power to forgive sins, as demonstrated in Mark 2:5-7,

where He heals a paralytic and forgives his sins, leading the scribes to accuse Him of blasphemy because only God can forgive sins.

3. Revelation of the Father: Jesus, as the Son of God, perfectly reveals the Father to humanity. In John 14:9, Jesus tells Philip, "He who has seen Me has seen the Father." This statement underscores the idea that Jesus is the exact representation of God's nature, as described in Hebrews 1:3: "He is the radiance of His glory and the exact representation of His nature." Through Jesus, humanity encounters the fullness of God's character, love, and will.

2.4 The Son of God in the Synoptic Gospels

The Synoptic Gospels (Matthew, Mark, and Luke) provide numerous instances where Jesus is identified as the Son of God. In addition to the divine affirmations at His baptism and Transfiguration, demons frequently acknowledge Jesus as the Son of God, recognizing His authority over them (Matthew 8:29; Mark 3:11). This recognition by spiritual beings further attests to Jesus' divine status.

Moreover, the title "Son of God" is closely linked to Jesus' messianic role. In Matthew 16:16, Peter's confession, "You are the Christ, the Son of the living God," highlights the connection between Jesus' messianic mission and His divine sonship. Jesus affirms Peter's confession, stating that it was revealed to him by God the Father (Matthew 16:17), emphasizing the divine origin and truth of this title.

2.5 The Son of God in the Gospel of John

The Gospel of John places particular emphasis on Jesus as the Son of God. The prologue of John (John 1:1-18) introduces Jesus as the Word who was with God and was God, setting the stage for the unfolding revelation of

His divine sonship. Throughout the Gospel, Jesus refers to God as His Father, highlighting their unique relationship.

John 3:16, one of the most well-known verses in the Bible, encapsulates the significance of Jesus as the Son of God: "For God so loved the world that He gave His only begotten Son, that whoever believes in Him should not perish but have everlasting life." This verse underscores the sacrificial love of God in sending His Son and the salvific purpose of Jesus' mission.

In John 5:19-23, Jesus elaborates on His relationship with the Father, stating that He can do nothing by Himself but only what He sees the Father doing. He also asserts that the Father has entrusted all judgment to the Son so that all may honor the Son just as they honor the Father. This passage reveals the depth of the unity between the Father and the Son and the divine authority vested in Jesus.

2.6 Theological Implications of Jesus as the Son of God

Understanding Jesus as the Son of God carries profound theological implications:

1. Christology: The title "Son of God" is central to Christology, the study of the person and work of Christ. It affirms Jesus' divinity, His pre-existence, and His unique relationship with the Father. This understanding is vital for a correct interpretation of who Jesus is and what He accomplished through His life, death, and resurrection.

2. Salvation: Jesus' identity as the Son of God is directly connected to His ability to save. As the divine Son, He possesses the power to atone for sin, reconcile humanity to God, and grant eternal life. Only a Savior who is fully God can bridge the gap between a holy God and sinful humanity.

3. Trinitarian Doctrine: The title "Son of God" is integral to the doctrine of the Trinity. It highlights the distinction of persons within the Godhead while maintaining the unity of essence. Jesus' sonship demonstrates the relational aspect of the Trinity, where the Father, Son, and Holy Spirit exist in perfect harmony and love.

4. Worship and Devotion: Recognizing Jesus as the Son of God compels believers to worship Him as Lord and God. The acknowledgment of His divine sonship leads to a life of devotion, obedience, and reverence, as believers respond to the revelation of who He is.

2.7 Conclusion

The title "Son of God" is not merely a descriptor but a profound affirmation of Jesus' divine nature and unique relationship with God the Father. It encapsulates the essence of who Jesus is—eternally begotten, possessing divine authority, and perfectly revealing the Father to humanity. This understanding is essential for a full appreciation of Jesus' identity and His role in the salvation of the world.

As we reflect on Jesus as the Son of God, we are invited to deepen our faith and devotion, recognizing that in Him, we encounter the fullness of God's love, grace, and truth. This title, rich in meaning and significance, stands at the heart of Christian belief, shaping our understanding of Jesus and our relationship with Him.

The Purpose of the Book

3.1 Introduction

The divinity of Jesus Christ is the cornerstone of Christian faith. It is not merely a theological concept but the very foundation upon which the entirety of Christianity is built. This book aims to explore and affirm the divinity of Jesus Christ, as well as to demonstrate why recognizing and understanding this truth is crucial for believers. By delving into the biblical, historical, and theological aspects of Jesus' divine nature, this book seeks to strengthen the reader's faith and deepen their relationship with Christ.

3.2 The Centrality of Jesus' Divinity in Christian Faith

At the heart of Christianity lies the belief that Jesus Christ is not just a prophet, teacher, or moral example but the incarnate Son of God—fully divine and fully human. This belief distinguishes Christianity from all other religions and philosophies. It is what makes Christianity unique and what gives it its transformative power.

The significance of Jesus' divinity is evident throughout the New Testament. The Gospels, the writings of Paul, and the teachings of the early Church all emphasize that Jesus is God in the flesh, come to redeem humanity. This understanding is crucial because it directly affects how Christians view salvation, worship, and their relationship with God.

If Jesus were merely a human being, even an extraordinarily good one, His death on the cross would not have the power to atone for the sins of the world. It is precisely because Jesus is divine that His sacrifice is sufficient to cover the sins of all people, providing a way for humanity to be reconciled to God. The recognition of Jesus' divinity is, therefore, essential for understanding the nature of salvation.

Moreover, the divinity of Jesus informs the Christian practice of worship. Christians do not merely follow the teachings of a wise man; they worship Jesus as Lord and God. The early Church was willing to suffer persecution and martyrdom for the confession that "Jesus is Lord," a confession that would be meaningless if Jesus were not divine. The act of worship is directed toward God alone, and the fact that Jesus is worshiped by Christians throughout history affirms His divine status.

3.3 The Role of the Holy Spirit in Revealing Jesus' Divinity

The Holy Spirit plays a crucial role in revealing the divinity of Jesus to believers. As Jesus Himself stated, the Spirit will "guide you into all truth" and "will take of what is Mine and declare it to you" (John 16:13-14). The Spirit's work is to glorify Christ and to lead believers into a deeper understanding of His nature and mission.

Recognizing Jesus' divinity is not merely an intellectual exercise; it is a spiritual revelation that comes through the work of the Holy Spirit. This book seeks to align with the Spirit's work by providing a biblical and theological framework that supports and deepens the reader's understanding of Jesus' divine nature.

The purpose of this book, therefore, is not just to present doctrinal truths but to facilitate a spiritual encounter with the living Christ. Through the study of Scripture and the guidance of the Holy Spirit, readers are invited to see Jesus as He truly is—the eternal Son of God, worthy of all honor, glory, and praise.

3.4 Strengthening Faith Through Understanding

One of the primary purposes of this book is to strengthen the faith of believers by providing a clear and comprehensive understanding of Jesus' divinity. In a world where faith is often challenged by skepticism, secularism, and alternative spiritualities, it is essential for Christians to be firmly rooted in the truth of who Jesus is.

A robust understanding of Jesus' divinity equips believers to withstand the pressures and doubts that may arise in their spiritual journey. It also enables them to confidently share their faith with others, providing answers to questions and objections that may be raised by those who do not yet know Christ.

Furthermore, understanding Jesus' divinity deepens the believer's appreciation for the love and grace of God. The realization that the Creator of the universe took on human flesh, lived among us, and died for our sins is a profound truth that should inspire awe and gratitude. It reminds us of the lengths to which God has gone to redeem us and how much He values each of us.

3.5 Addressing Contemporary Challenges to Jesus' Divinity

In contemporary society, there are many challenges to the belief in Jesus' divinity. Some view Jesus as merely a historical figure, a moral teacher, or a revolutionary leader. Others question the reliability of the biblical accounts or reinterpret them in ways that diminish or deny His divine nature.

This book seeks to address these challenges by presenting a clear and compelling case for Jesus' divinity based on biblical evidence, historical context, and theological reflection. By engaging with these issues, the book aims to equip believers with the knowledge and confidence they need to stand firm in their faith and to articulate their beliefs in a way that is both intellectually credible and spiritually enriching.

In addition to addressing external challenges, the book also seeks to help believers overcome internal doubts and struggles. Many Christians may experience moments of uncertainty or confusion about their faith, particularly in a culture that is increasingly skeptical of religious claims. By providing a deeper understanding of who Jesus is, this book aims to help believers navigate these challenges and emerge with a stronger, more resilient faith.

3.6 The Transformative Power of Recognizing Jesus' Divinity

Finally, this book is written with the conviction that recognizing Jesus' divinity has the power to transform lives. When we understand that Jesus is not just a figure from history but the living God who is actively involved in our lives, it changes everything.

Recognizing Jesus' divinity leads to a deeper commitment to following Him. It challenges us to live lives that reflect His lordship, to pursue holiness, and to love others as He has loved us. It also brings comfort and assurance, knowing that the one we follow is not just a human leader but the eternal Son of God, who has conquered sin and death and who reigns as Lord of all.

Moreover, recognizing Jesus' divinity opens up the possibility of a personal relationship with God. Through Jesus, we are invited into the very life of the Trinity, to know God as Father, Son, and Holy Spirit. This relationship is the source of all true joy, peace, and fulfillment, and it is available to all who acknowledge Jesus as Lord and Savior.

3.7 Conclusion

The purpose of this book is to affirm, explore, and deepen the reader's understanding of the divinity of Jesus Christ. This truth is central to the Christian faith, shaping our understanding of salvation, worship, and our relationship with God. By providing a biblical, historical, and theological foundation for this belief, the book aims to strengthen the faith of believers, address contemporary challenges, and facilitate a deeper spiritual encounter with Christ.

As you read and reflect on the contents of this book, may the Holy Spirit guide you into all truth, and may you come to a fuller recognition of Jesus Christ as the eternal Son of God, the Savior of the world, and the Lord of all creation.

CHAPTER 08

LINKING OLD TESTAMENT PROPHECY TO JESUS

1. Introduction

The New Testament writers consistently link Jesus Christ to the messianic prophecies of the Old Testament, and one of the most significant of these prophecies is found in Jeremiah 23:5-6, which speaks of the "Branch of Righteousness" from the line of David. For the early Christians, understanding Jesus as the fulfillment of these prophecies was crucial to affirming His identity as the Messiah and the Son of God. The title "The Lord our righteousness" ascribed to this future king in Jeremiah's prophecy resonated deeply with the early church, as they saw in Jesus the divine Savior who would bring salvation, righteousness, and the fulfillment of God's promises.

In this chapter, we will explore how the New Testament writers directly and indirectly linked Jeremiah's prophecy of the "Branch of Righteousness" to the life, ministry, and redemptive work of Jesus. By doing so, we will better understand how early Christians viewed Jesus not just as a continuation of Israel's hope but as the ultimate fulfillment of the messianic expectations laid out in the Old Testament.

2. Jesus as the Davidic King

One of the central themes of Jeremiah's prophecy is the promise of a righteous king from the line of David. In Jeremiah 23:5-6, the Lord declares that He will raise up a "righteous Branch" from David's line, signaling the continuation of the Davidic dynasty and the fulfillment of God's covenant with David. The New Testament writers explicitly identify Jesus as this Davidic king, making it clear that He is the long-awaited Messiah who fulfills the promises of the Old Testament.

2.1 The Genealogies of Jesus

Both the Gospels of Matthew and Luke take great care to trace Jesus' genealogy back to David, affirming His royal lineage and His rightful claim to the Davidic throne. In Matthew 1:1, the genealogy opens with the declaration, "The book of the genealogy of Jesus Christ, the son of David, the son of Abraham," immediately linking Jesus to the covenantal promises made to both Abraham and David.

The genealogy in Matthew 1:6 specifically mentions David: "And Jesse the father of David the king. And David was the father of Solomon by the wife of Uriah." This genealogical record not only affirms Jesus' legal claim to the Davidic throne through Joseph but also emphasizes His connection to the prophecies of the Davidic line, including the one found in Jeremiah 23.

Similarly, in Luke 1:32-33, the angel Gabriel announces to Mary that her son will fulfill the role of the Davidic king:

> "He will be great and will be called the Son of the Most High. And the Lord God will give him the throne of his father David, and he will reign over the house of Jacob forever, and of his kingdom there will be no end." (ESV)

This passage directly ties Jesus' kingship to the promises made in the Davidic Covenant (2 Samuel 7:12-16) and echoes Jeremiah's prophecy that the Branch of David will rule with wisdom, righteousness, and justice.

2.2 Jesus Proclaimed as the King of Israel

Throughout the New Testament, Jesus is repeatedly identified as the King of Israel, a fulfillment of the messianic expectation for a Davidic ruler. In John 1:49, Nathanael proclaims Jesus as the King of Israel:

> "Nathanael answered him, 'Rabbi, you are the Son of God! You are the King of Israel!'" (ESV)

By referring to Jesus as the King of Israel, Nathanael acknowledges Jesus' rightful place as the descendant of David and the fulfillment of Jeremiah's prophecy about the Branch of Righteousness.

Moreover, during Jesus' triumphal entry into Jerusalem, the crowds hailed Him as the promised king from David's line. In Matthew 21:9, we read:

> "And the crowds that went before him and that followed him were shouting, 'Hosanna to the Son of David! Blessed is he who comes in the name of the Lord! Hosanna in the highest!'" (ESV)

This moment, celebrated on Palm Sunday, is significant because it shows the people of Jerusalem recognizing Jesus as the Davidic king, directly tying their hope in the Messiah to the Old Testament promises, including those found in Jeremiah 23.

3. Jesus as the Righteous Branch

In Jeremiah 23:5, the future Davidic king is described as a "righteous Branch" who will reign with wisdom and execute justice. For early Christians, Jesus perfectly embodied the righteousness and justice prophesied by Jeremiah, and they often referred to Him in ways that reflect this understanding.

3.1 Jesus as the Embodiment of Righteousness

The righteousness of the Branch in Jeremiah's prophecy is not merely a moral quality but reflects divine righteousness. Jesus is seen as the fulfillment of this aspect of the prophecy, as He embodies perfect righteousness and offers that righteousness to humanity. In the New Testament, Jesus is frequently associated with righteousness, both in His teachings and in the salvation He offers.

In 1 Corinthians 1:30, Paul speaks of Jesus as the source of righteousness for believers:

> "And because of him you are in Christ Jesus, who became to us wisdom from God, righteousness and sanctification and redemption." (ESV)

This passage ties Jesus' role directly to the prophecy of the righteous Branch, as He is identified as the one through whom God's righteousness is made available to humanity. Christians believe that through faith in Jesus, they receive the righteousness that was prophesied in Jeremiah 23.

Similarly, in Romans 3:22, Paul writes:

> "The righteousness of God through faith in Jesus Christ for all who believe." (ESV)

For Paul and other early Christians, the righteousness that the Branch brings is fulfilled in Jesus, whose life, death, and resurrection provide the means by which people are made right with God.

3.2 Jesus and the Ministry of Justice and Salvation

Jeremiah's prophecy also speaks of the Branch who will "do justice and righteousness in the land" and bring salvation to Judah and Israel. Throughout His ministry, Jesus exemplified justice and salvation, not only through His teaching but through His redemptive work on the cross.

In Luke 4:18-19, at the beginning of His public ministry, Jesus announces His mission, quoting from the prophet Isaiah:

> "The Spirit of the Lord is upon me, because he has anointed me to proclaim good news to the poor. He has sent me to proclaim liberty to the captives and recovering of sight to the blind, to set at liberty those who are oppressed, to proclaim the year of the Lord's favor." (ESV)

Here, Jesus emphasizes justice for the oppressed and salvation for the captives, themes that resonate with Jeremiah's prophecy about the righteous Branch. By healing the sick, raising the dead, and offering forgiveness to sinners, Jesus demonstrated the justice and salvation that the Messiah was expected to bring.

4. Jesus as "The Lord Our Righteousness"

One of the most powerful aspects of Jeremiah's prophecy is the title given to the Branch: "The LORD our righteousness" (YHWH Tsidkenu). This title implies both divine and redemptive qualities. For early Christians, this name was a clear indication of Jesus' divine identity and His role in bringing about the righteousness of God.

4.1 The Divine Identity of Jesus

The title "The LORD our righteousness" uses the divine name YHWH, which is significant because it directly associates the Branch with God Himself. In Christian theology, this title is seen as an affirmation of Jesus' divinity. The New Testament writers emphasize that Jesus is not only a descendant of David but also the incarnate Son of God, fully divine and fully human.

In John 1:1, 14, we read about Jesus' divine nature:

> "In the beginning was the Word, and the Word was with God, and the Word was God... And the Word became flesh and dwelt among us, and we have seen his glory, glory as of the only Son from the Father, full of grace and truth." (ESV)

By describing Jesus as "the Word" who "was God" and "became flesh," John affirms the belief that Jesus, as the Messiah, fulfills the divine aspect of Jeremiah's prophecy. He is YHWH Tsidkenu—the Lord who embodies and brings righteousness.

4.2 Jesus as the Provider of Righteousness

For early Christians, one of the key ways Jesus fulfilled the prophecy of the Branch was by providing righteousness to all who believe in Him. This is a central theme in Paul's writings, where he repeatedly emphasizes that righteousness comes through faith in Christ, not through works of the law.

In Philippians 3:9, Paul writes:

> "And be found in him, not having a righteousness of my own that comes from the law, but that which comes through faith in Christ, the righteousness from God that depends on faith." (ESV)

This idea of being made righteous through faith in Jesus is central to Christian soteriology, the doctrine of salvation. Christians believe that through Jesus, they receive the righteousness of God, which was promised in the Old Testament. This aligns directly with Jeremiah's prophecy that the Branch would be called "The LORD our righteousness," as Jesus is understood to be the one who provides the righteousness necessary for salvation.

5. Conclusion: Jesus as the Fulfillment of Jeremiah's Prophecy

For the New Testament writers, the connection between Jeremiah

's prophecy of the "Branch of Righteousness" and the life and ministry of Jesus is clear. Jesus is seen as the Davidic king who fulfills the promises made to Israel, not merely as a political leader but as the divine Savior who embodies righteousness and offers it to all who believe.

Jesus fulfills the divine title "The LORD our righteousness" through His incarnation, life, death, and resurrection, providing the means by which humanity is reconciled to God. In this way, Christians view Jesus as the ultimate fulfillment of Jeremiah's prophecy, the righteous Branch who brings salvation and peace to Israel and the entire world.

The New Covenant

1. Introduction: The Promise of a New Covenant

In Jeremiah 31:31-34, one of the most profound promises of the Old Testament is declared: the coming of a New Covenant between God and His people. This covenant, unlike the one made at Sinai, would be internal and transformative, written on the hearts of God's people rather than on tablets of stone. For Christians, this passage holds immense theological significance because they believe that Jesus Christ instituted this New Covenant through His life, death, and resurrection. The New Testament, particularly the Book of Hebrews, emphasizes that Jesus is the mediator of this New Covenant, fulfilling the promises made through Jeremiah and bringing about a new era in the relationship between God and humanity.

The concept of the New Covenant marks a turning point in the biblical narrative, transitioning from the external regulations of the Mosaic Law to the internal transformation that comes through the work of the Holy Spirit. In this chapter, we will explore the significance of the New Covenant as presented in Jeremiah, its fulfillment in the life and work of Jesus, and how the New Testament writers understood this covenant in relation to the broader story of salvation.

2. The Old Covenant: Its Nature and Limitations

To fully appreciate the significance of the New Covenant, it is essential to understand the nature of the Old Covenant, which was established between God and the people of Israel at Mount Sinai. This covenant, often referred to as the Mosaic Covenant, was based on the Law that God gave to Moses, which included the Ten Commandments and the various ceremonial, moral, and civil laws that governed Israel's relationship with God and one another.

2.1 The Covenant at Sinai

The Old Covenant was a binding agreement that God made with Israel after delivering them from slavery in Egypt. In Exodus 19:5-6, God makes the terms of the covenant clear:

> "Now therefore, if you will indeed obey my voice and keep my covenant, you shall be my treasured possession among all peoples, for all the earth is mine; and you shall be to me a kingdom of priests and a holy nation." (ESV)

The covenant was conditional, dependent on Israel's obedience to God's laws. Israel was called to be a holy nation, set apart from other peoples, and their continued blessing and relationship with God depended on their adherence to the covenant.

2.2 The Law and the Covenant

The heart of the Old Covenant was the Law, which God gave to Israel as both a guide for righteous living and a means to maintain fellowship with Him. However, the Law also revealed humanity's inability to fully live up to God's standards. Time and again, Israel failed to keep the terms of the covenant, turning to idolatry and disobedience. The prophet Jeremiah repeatedly laments Israel's faithlessness, describing how they have broken the covenant made with God.

In Jeremiah 11:10, God says:

> "They have turned back to the iniquities of their forefathers, who refused to hear my words. They have gone after other gods to serve them. The house of Israel and the house of Judah have broken my covenant that I made with their fathers." (ESV)

This failure highlighted the limitations of the Old Covenant. While the Law was perfect and holy, it could not transform the hearts of the people. Israel's continual disobedience revealed the need for a deeper, more transformative covenant—one that would address the internal condition of the human heart.

3. The Prophecy of the New Covenant

Against the backdrop of Israel's failure to keep the Old Covenant, Jeremiah offers a remarkable prophecy of hope and renewal. In Jeremiah 31:31-34, God speaks of a New Covenant that will not be like the one made at Sinai but will bring about a profound internal transformation in His people:

> "Behold, the days are coming, declares the LORD, when I will make a new covenant with the house of Israel and the house of Judah, not like the covenant that I made with their fathers on the day when I took them by the hand to bring them out of the land of Egypt, my covenant that they broke, though I was their husband, declares the LORD. But this is the covenant that I will make with the house of Israel after those days, declares the LORD: I will put my law within them, and I will write it on their hearts. And I will be their God, and they shall be my people. And no longer shall each one teach his neighbor and each his brother, saying, 'Know the LORD,' for they shall all know me, from the least of them to the greatest, declares the LORD. For I will forgive their iniquity, and I will remember their sin no more." (ESV)

This passage is revolutionary because it shifts the focus from external laws and rituals to an internal, heart-centered relationship between God and His people. The key features of this New Covenant are:

3.1 An Internal Law

Unlike the Old Covenant, where the law was written on stone tablets, the New Covenant promises that God's law will be written on the hearts of His people. This implies a transformation of the inner person, where obedience to God is no longer an external obligation but flows from a renewed heart. This internalization of God's law points to the work of the Holy Spirit, who, according to Christian theology, indwells believers and empowers them to live in obedience to God.

3.2 A Personal Relationship with God

In the New Covenant, God promises that all His people will know Him personally. This knowledge is not merely intellectual but relational and experiential. In the Old Covenant, the people relied on priests and mediators to represent them before God, but the New Covenant promises direct access to God for all His people, "from the least of them to the greatest." This democratization of access to God reflects the intimate relationship God desires to have with His people.

3.3 Forgiveness of Sins

One of the most significant aspects of the New Covenant is the promise of forgiveness: "For I will forgive their iniquity, and I will remember their sin no more." Under the Old Covenant, forgiveness was temporary and required repeated sacrifices. But in the New Covenant, God promises complete and lasting forgiveness of sins, a promise that Christians believe is fulfilled through the sacrifice of Jesus Christ.

4. The Fulfillment of the New Covenant in Jesus

Christians believe that Jesus Christ is the mediator of the New Covenant, fulfilling the prophecy in Jeremiah through His life, death, and resurrection. The New Testament repeatedly identifies Jesus as the one who brings the New Covenant into reality, and His sacrifice on the cross is seen as the means by which the New Covenant is established.

4.1 Jesus' Institution of the New Covenant

The clearest connection between Jesus and the New Covenant is found in the accounts of the Last Supper, where Jesus explicitly refers to His impending death as the institution of the New Covenant. In Luke 22:20, Jesus says:

> "And likewise the cup after they had eaten, saying, 'This cup that is poured out for you is the new covenant in my blood.'" (ESV)

By referring to His blood as the basis of the New Covenant, Jesus connects His sacrificial death with the promises made in Jeremiah 31. His death on the cross is understood by Christians as the ultimate act of atonement, providing the forgiveness of sins promised in the New Covenant.

4.2 The Book of Hebrews and the New Covenant

The Book of Hebrews provides the most extensive theological reflection on the New Covenant and its fulfillment in Jesus. Hebrews portrays Jesus as the great High Priest and the mediator of a better covenant, one that surpasses the Old Covenant in every way. In Hebrews 8:6-7, we read:

> "But as it is, Christ has obtained a ministry that is as much more excellent than the old as the covenant he mediates is better, since it is enacted on better promises. For if that first covenant had been faultless, there would have been no occasion to look for a second." (ESV)

The author of Hebrews directly quotes Jeremiah 31:31-34 in Hebrews 8:8-12, arguing that the New Covenant has been fulfilled in Jesus and that His once-for-all sacrifice replaces the repeated animal sacrifices of the Old Covenant. Through Jesus, believers experience the internal transformation and forgiveness that Jeremiah promised.

4.3 The Holy Spirit and the New Covenant

The promise of an internal law written on the hearts of God's people is fulfilled in Christian theology through the indwelling of the Holy Spirit. In the New Testament, the Holy Spirit is described as the agent of transformation who enables believers to live according to God's will. In 2 Corinthians 3:3, Paul writes:

> "And you show that you are a letter from Christ delivered by us, written not with ink but with the Spirit of the living God, not on tablets of stone but on tablets of human hearts." (ESV)

This imagery directly echoes Jeremiah's prophecy, where God promises to write His law on the hearts of His people. The Holy Spirit plays a central role in the New Covenant, enabling believers to live in a new relationship with God, marked by obedience, intimacy, and forgiveness.

5. The New Covenant and Christian Life

For Christians, living under the New Covenant means experiencing a transformed relationship with God, characterized by forgiveness, direct access to God, and the indwelling presence of the Holy Spirit. The New Covenant redefines what it means to be in covenant with God, shifting the focus from external rituals to a heart-oriented faith.

5.1 Forgiveness and Reconciliation

The New Covenant, as established through Jesus, offers full and final forgiveness of sins. This forgiveness is not contingent on repeated sacrifices, as in the Old Covenant, but is secured through the once-for-all sacrifice of Jesus. Christians believe that through faith in Jesus, they are reconciled to God and can live in the assurance of God's grace and mercy.

5.2 The Law Written on Hearts

The internalization of God's law is one of the hallmarks of the New Covenant. Christians believe that the Holy Spirit empowers them to live in accordance with God's will, not out of mere obligation but out of a transformed heart. This inward transformation reflects the deep intimacy of the New Covenant relationship, where obedience to God is an act of love and worship rather than external compliance.

5.3 The Universal Scope of the New Covenant

While Jeremiah's prophecy was initially directed at the house of Israel and Judah, the New Covenant is understood in Christian theology to extend beyond ethnic Israel to include all people. Through Jesus, the New Covenant is offered to all nations, fulfilling God's promise to bless all the families of the earth. As Paul writes in Galatians 3:28-29:

> "There is neither Jew nor Greek, there is neither slave nor free, there is no male and female, for you are all one in Christ Jesus. And if you are Christ's, then you are Abraham's offspring, heirs according to promise." (ESV)

This universal aspect of the New Covenant reflects the expansion of God's plan of salvation, where all who believe in Jesus are brought into the family of God and experience the blessings of the New Covenant.

6. Conclusion: The Fulfillment of the New Covenant in Jesus

The prophecy of the New Covenant in Jeremiah 31:31-34 is one of the most significant promises in the Old Testament, offering hope for a future in which God's people would experience a transformed relationship with Him. For Christians, this promise is fulfilled in Jesus Christ, who established the New Covenant through His death and resurrection. Jesus, as the mediator of the New Covenant, brings forgiveness of sins, writes God's law on the hearts of believers, and offers a direct, personal relationship with God.

The New Covenant represents a profound shift in the way humanity relates to God, moving from external regulations to an internal transformation through the Holy

Spirit. For Christians, living under the New Covenant means experiencing the grace and mercy of God through Jesus Christ, and it provides the assurance of forgiveness, intimacy with God, and the promise of eternal life. Thus, the New Covenant stands as a central pillar of Christian theology, embodying the fulfillment of God's redemptive plan for humanity.

The Old Covenant vs. The New Covenant

1. Introduction: The Shift from the Old Covenant to the New Covenant

The Old Covenant, often referred to as the Mosaic Covenant, is central to the history of Israel's relationship with God. This covenant, established at Mount Sinai, laid the foundation for how the Israelites were to live, worship, and relate to God. However, as the Old Testament narratives unfold, it becomes clear that the Mosaic Covenant, while holy and good, had significant limitations due to human sinfulness. These limitations created the need for a New Covenant, one that would address the shortcomings of the old system and provide a lasting solution to humanity's separation from God.

In Jeremiah 31:31-34, the prophet foretells a New Covenant that would be different from the one made with the Israelites at Sinai. This New Covenant would address the inherent weaknesses of the Old Covenant and establish a deeper, more intimate relationship between God and His people. For Christians, this New Covenant is fulfilled through Jesus Christ, whose life, death, and resurrection bring about a transformative relationship with God that transcends the limitations of the Mosaic Covenant.

In this chapter, we will explore the key differences between the Old and New Covenants, the limitations of the

Mosaic Law, and the theological reasons for the establishment of the New Covenant.

2. The Old Covenant: Structure and Purpose

2.1 The Mosaic Covenant

The Old Covenant was formally established between God and the people of Israel at Mount Sinai after their exodus from Egypt. It is referred to as the Mosaic Covenant because Moses was the mediator between God and the Israelites during this pivotal event. The essence of this covenant was captured in the giving of the Law, which included the Ten Commandments, as well as various ceremonial, moral, and civil regulations designed to govern Israel's relationship with God and one another.

In Exodus 19:5-6, God laid out the terms of this covenant:

> "Now therefore, if you will indeed obey my voice and keep my covenant, you shall be my treasured possession among all peoples, for all the earth is mine; and you shall be to me a kingdom of priests and a holy nation." (ESV)

This covenant was conditional and based on obedience. Israel was called to be a holy nation, set apart from the surrounding peoples. In return for their obedience, God promised to bless them, protect them, and dwell among them.

2.2 The Purpose of the Mosaic Law

The Law given through Moses had several key purposes:

- To Reflect God's Holiness: The Law was a reflection of God's holiness and righteousness. It was designed to set Israel apart from other nations as a people who lived according to God's standards.

- To Regulate Worship and Life: The ceremonial and sacrificial aspects of the Law regulated how the Israelites were to worship God. It also provided guidelines for living in community, promoting justice, mercy, and love toward one another.

- To Serve as a Covenant Sign: The Law served as the sign of the covenant between God and Israel. By keeping the Law, the Israelites demonstrated their loyalty and commitment to God.

- To Expose Sin: The Law also had the function of exposing sin. Paul writes in Romans 7:7 that the Law revealed the true nature of sin: "Yet if it had not been for the law, I would not have known sin. For I would not have known what it is to covet if the law had not said, 'You shall not covet.'" (ESV)

While the Mosaic Law was good and served as a guide for righteous living, it had inherent limitations due to human sinfulness. These limitations underscored the need for a New Covenant that would go beyond the external regulations of the Law.

3. The Limitations of the Old Covenant

Despite its divine origin, the Old Covenant had several limitations that made it ineffective as a permanent solution to humanity's problem of sin and estrangement from God. The primary limitations of the Mosaic Covenant can be summarized as follows:

3.1 External Law

One of the most significant limitations of the Old Covenant was its external nature. The Mosaic Law was written on stone tablets and required adherence to external rules and rituals. While the Law could guide behavior, it could not change the human heart. The Law revealed what righteousness looked like, but it did not have the power to enable people to live righteously from within.

Jeremiah highlighted this problem in Jeremiah 17:9, where he describes the condition of the human heart:

> "The heart is deceitful above all things, and desperately sick; who can understand it?" (ESV)

This deep-rooted sinfulness meant that the people of Israel were incapable of fully keeping the Law, even though they might strive to follow its precepts externally.

3.2 The Problem of Human Disobedience

The Old Covenant was based on conditional promises—if Israel obeyed, they would experience blessings, but if they disobeyed, they would face curses and punishment (Deuteronomy 28). However, Israel's history is one of repeated disobedience and covenant breaking. Time and again, the people turned away from God to worship idols and follow their own desires.

Jeremiah points out the failure of the people to keep the covenant in Jeremiah 11:10:

> "They have turned back to the iniquities of their forefathers, who refused to hear my words. They have gone after other gods to serve them. The house of Israel and the house of Judah have broken my covenant that I made with their fathers." (ESV)

The repeated disobedience of Israel demonstrated the inadequacy of the Old Covenant to produce lasting faithfulness to God. The people's inability to uphold their end of the covenant highlighted the need for a new approach—one that addressed the problem of human sinfulness more effectively.

3.3 Temporary Sacrifices for Sin

Another major limitation of the Old Covenant was its sacrificial system. Under the Mosaic Law, animal sacrifices were required to atone for the sins of the people. However, these sacrifices were temporary and needed to be repeated continually. The blood of animals could not fully cleanse people from sin but only provided a temporary covering. In Hebrews 10:1, the writer explains:

> "For since the law has but a shadow of the good things to come instead of the true form of these realities, it can never, by the same sacrifices that are continually offered every year, make perfect those who draw near." (ESV)

The sacrificial system of the Old Covenant pointed forward to a greater sacrifice—one that would provide permanent forgiveness and cleansing from sin.

3.4 Lack of Internal Transformation

Perhaps the most significant limitation of the Old Covenant was its inability to transform the hearts of the people. While the Law could instruct and reveal sin, it could not provide the power to live in true obedience to God. This lack of internal transformation meant that the people were constantly falling into cycles of disobedience and repentance, never fully able to maintain the covenant relationship with God.

As a result of these limitations, the Old Covenant was unable to bring about the full restoration and redemption that humanity needed. The Law was good, but it could not overcome the problem of sin at its root. This reality created the need for a New Covenant—one that would address the internal condition of the human heart and provide a lasting solution to sin and separation from God.

4. The New Covenant: Addressing the Limitations of the Old

The New Covenant, as prophesied by Jeremiah, was designed to address the limitations of the Old Covenant and provide a permanent, transformative solution to humanity's problem of sin. In Jeremiah 31:31-34, God promises to establish a New Covenant that would fundamentally change the relationship between God and His people:

> "Behold, the days are coming, declares the LORD, when I will make a new covenant with the house of Israel and the house of Judah… For this is the covenant that I will make with the house of Israel after those days, declares the LORD: I will put my law within them, and I will write it on their hearts. And I will be their God, and they shall be my people… For I will forgive their iniquity, and I will remember their sin no more." (ESV)

4.1 The Law Written on Hearts

One of the key features of the New Covenant is that God's law would no longer be external but would be written on the hearts of His people. This promise signifies a profound internal transformation, where obedience to God would come from a changed heart rather than mere external conformity. The New Covenant addresses the problem of the human heart by providing the internal renewal necessary for true obedience to God's will.

In Christian theology, this internal transformation is accomplished through the indwelling of the Holy Spirit. Paul explains in 2 Corinthians 3:3:

> "And you show that you are a letter from Christ delivered by us, written not with ink but with the Spirit of the living God, not on tablets of stone but on tablets of human hearts." (ESV)

The Holy Spirit empowers believers to live in accordance with God's will, fulfilling the promise of the New Covenant that the law would be written on their hearts.

4.2 Personal Knowledge of God

Another feature of the New Covenant is the promise of a personal relationship with God. Under the Old Covenant, access to God was mediated through priests, and the people often felt distant from God. However, in the New Covenant, God promises that "they shall all know me, from the least of them to the greatest." This knowledge is relational and intimate, reflecting the closeness that God desires to have with His people.

This personal relationship with God is made possible through Jesus Christ, who, as the mediator of the New Covenant, provides direct access to the Father. In Hebrews 4:16, believers are encouraged to approach God with confidence:

> "Let us then with confidence draw near to the throne of grace, that we may receive mercy and find grace to help in time of need." (ESV)

This access to God is one of the central benefits of the New Covenant, where every believer can experience a direct, personal relationship with their Creator.

4.3 Complete Forgiveness of Sins

Perhaps the most significant aspect of the New Covenant is the promise of complete and lasting forgiveness of sins. In Jeremiah 31:34, God declares, "For I will forgive their iniquity, and I will remember their sin no more." This forgiveness is not temporary, as it was under the Old Covenant, but is permanent and complete.

Christians believe that this forgiveness is made possible through the sacrificial death of Jesus Christ. As the ultimate sacrifice, Jesus' death on the cross provides atonement for sin once and for all. In Hebrews 10:12, it is written:

> "But when Christ had offered for all time a single sacrifice for sins, he sat down at the right hand of God." (ESV)

Jesus' sacrifice fulfills the requirements of the Old Covenant's sacrificial system and brings about the full and final forgiveness of sins, as promised in the New Covenant.

5. The Need for the New Covenant

The limitations of the Old Covenant, combined with humanity's inability to live in perfect obedience to God's law, created the need for a New Covenant. The Mosaic Law, while good and holy, could not address the fundamental problem of sin and the need for internal transformation. The New Covenant, however, provides the solution by offering:

- Internal Transformation: Through the work of the Holy Spirit, believers are transformed from the inside out, enabling them to live in true obedience to God.

- Direct Access to God: The New Covenant offers a personal relationship with God, where all people can know Him intimately and experience His presence.

- Complete Forgiveness: Through the sacrifice of Jesus Christ, the New Covenant brings complete and lasting forgiveness of sins, eliminating the need for repeated sacrifices.

In Christian theology, the New Covenant is understood as the fulfillment of God's redemptive plan, where the limitations of the Old Covenant are overcome, and the relationship between God and humanity is restored through Jesus Christ.

6. Conclusion: The Superiority of the New Covenant

The Old Covenant, established at Sinai, served an essential purpose in revealing God's holiness and exposing the problem of human sinfulness. However, its limitations—external regulations, human disobedience, and temporary sacrifices—necessitated a New Covenant, one that would address the root problem of sin and provide a permanent solution. The New Covenant, as prophesied by Jeremiah and fulfilled through Jesus Christ, surpasses the Old Covenant in every way. It offers internal transformation, personal knowledge of God, and complete forgiveness of sins, bringing about a restored relationship between God and humanity.

For Christians, the New Covenant represents the culmination of God's plan to redeem His people, offering a way of salvation that is not based on human effort but on the grace of God through Jesus Christ. In this way, the New Covenant fulfills the hopes and promises of the Old Testament and brings about a new era of peace, righteousness, and reconciliation with God.

Jesus and the New Covenant

1. Introduction: Jesus as the Fulfillment of the New Covenant

The New Covenant prophesied by Jeremiah in Jeremiah 31:31-34 represents a transformative shift in the relationship between God and His people. Unlike the Old Covenant, which was based on external laws and sacrifices, the New Covenant promised internal transformation, personal knowledge of God, and complete forgiveness of sins. For Christians, the life, death, and resurrection of Jesus Christ mark the fulfillment of this prophecy. Through His teachings, sacrificial death on the cross, and resurrection, Jesus inaugurated the New Covenant, bringing about the spiritual renewal that Jeremiah foretold.

This chapter will explore how Jesus' ministry, death, and resurrection fulfilled Jeremiah's prophecy of the New Covenant, transforming the relationship between God and humanity and establishing a new era of salvation, grace, and redemption.

2. Jesus' Teachings: The Kingdom of God and the Internalization of the Law

One of the key features of the New Covenant prophesied by Jeremiah was the promise that God's law would be written on the hearts of His people rather than merely being external rules written on stone. Jesus' teachings during His earthly ministry emphasized this shift from external obedience to internal transformation. He frequently taught that true righteousness comes from within and that the heart must be aligned with God's will.

2.1 The Sermon on the Mount: Internalizing the Law

In the Sermon on the Mount (Matthew 5-7), Jesus reinterpreted the Mosaic Law in a way that internalized its demands, emphasizing the spirit of the law rather than mere external adherence. Jesus did not abolish the Old Covenant law but fulfilled and deepened its meaning by calling for righteousness that exceeds the external observance of rules.

For example, in Matthew 5:21-22, Jesus says:

> "You have heard that it was said to those of old, 'You shall not murder; and whoever murders will be liable to judgment.' But I say to you that everyone who is angry with his brother will be liable to judgment." (ESV)

Here, Jesus highlights that it is not just the act of murder that violates God's will but the internal attitude of anger. Similarly, in Matthew 5:27-28, He extends the commandment against adultery to include even lustful thoughts. Jesus' teachings emphasized that the true fulfillment of the law involves a transformation of the heart—precisely what Jeremiah's New Covenant promised.

This internalization of the law is further reflected in Matthew 22:37-40, where Jesus summarizes the law as love for God and love for neighbor:

> "And he said to him, 'You shall love the Lord your God with all your heart and with all your soul and with all your mind. This is the great and first commandment. And a second is like it: You shall love your neighbor as yourself. On these two commandments depend all the Law and the Prophets.'" (ESV)

By teaching that the essence of the law is love—an internal orientation of the heart toward God and others—Jesus was laying the foundation for the New Covenant, where the law would be written on the hearts of believers through the work of the Holy Spirit.

2.2 The Kingdom of God: A New Relationship with God

Throughout His ministry, Jesus proclaimed the arrival of the Kingdom of God—a new era of God's rule in which people would live in direct, personal relationship with Him. This message ties closely to Jeremiah's prophecy that, under the New Covenant, "they shall all know me, from the least of them to the greatest" (Jeremiah 31:34).

Jesus' teachings emphasized that the Kingdom of God was not just a future political reality but a present spiritual reality that transforms the hearts and lives of those who enter into it. In Luke 17:20-21, Jesus says:

> "The kingdom of God is not coming in ways that can be observed, nor will they say, 'Look, here it is!' or 'There!' for behold, the kingdom of God is in the midst of you." (ESV)

By establishing the Kingdom of God in the hearts of His followers, Jesus initiated the New Covenant's promise of a personal, intimate relationship with God. This was a radical departure from the Old Covenant's focus on external rituals and regulations and marked the beginning of a new era in the relationship between God and His people.

3. Jesus' Death: The Sacrifice That Established the New Covenant

The New Covenant promised not only internal transformation but also the complete forgiveness of sins. This forgiveness is central to the New Covenant, as God declared through Jeremiah, "For I will forgive their iniquity, and I will remember their sin no more" (Jeremiah 31:34). Christians believe that this promise was fulfilled through Jesus' sacrificial death on the cross.

3.1 The Institution of the New Covenant at the Last Supper

The connection between Jesus' death and the New Covenant is most explicitly made during the Last Supper, where Jesus instituted the sacrament of the Eucharist (or Communion) and declared that His death would establish the New Covenant. In Luke 22:19-20, Jesus says:

> "And he took bread, and when he had given thanks, he broke it and gave it to them, saying, 'This is my body, which is given for you. Do this in remembrance of me.' And likewise the cup after they had eaten, saying, 'This cup that is poured out for you is the new covenant in my blood.'" (ESV)

By referring to His blood as the foundation of the New Covenant, Jesus directly connects His sacrificial death to the promises of forgiveness and transformation outlined in Jeremiah 31. Just as the Old Covenant was established through the blood of animal sacrifices (Exodus 24:8), the New Covenant is established through the shedding of Jesus' blood, which provides the final and perfect atonement for sin.

3.2 Jesus' Death as the Atonement for Sin

The New Covenant promised complete and lasting forgiveness of sins, something that the Old Covenant could not fully provide. Under the Old Covenant, the sacrificial system required repeated offerings of animals to temporarily cover the sins of the people. However, these sacrifices could never fully remove sin or cleanse the conscience. In contrast, Jesus' death on the cross is seen in Christian theology as the ultimate and final sacrifice that provides total forgiveness and reconciliation with God.

In Hebrews 9:12, the writer explains the significance of Jesus' sacrifice:

> "He entered once for all into the holy places, not by means of the blood of goats and calves but by means of his own blood, thus securing an eternal redemption." (ESV)

By offering His own life, Jesus accomplished what the Old Covenant sacrifices could not—permanent forgiveness and the removal of sin. This is why the writer of Hebrews refers to Jesus as the "mediator of a new covenant" (Hebrews 9:15), fulfilling Jeremiah's prophecy and providing a way for humanity to be restored to a right relationship with God.

4. Jesus' Resurrection: The Inauguration of New Life in the New Covenant

While Jesus' death is central to the establishment of the New Covenant, His resurrection is equally vital in bringing the promises of the New Covenant to full fruition. Jesus' resurrection not only vindicates His identity as the Messiah but also inaugurates the new life that believers experience under the New Covenant.

4.1 The Resurrection as the Confirmation of the New Covenant

Jesus' resurrection from the dead serves as a divine confirmation that His death was an acceptable and sufficient sacrifice for the forgiveness of sins. It is the ultimate proof that the promises of the New Covenant have been fulfilled. In Romans 4:25, Paul writes:

> "He was delivered up for our trespasses and raised for our justification." (ESV)

The resurrection is a declaration that Jesus' atoning work on the cross was successful, providing justification (or righteousness) for all who believe in Him. This justification is the fulfillment of the New Covenant promise that God's people would be made righteous and forgiven of their sins.

4.2 New Life in the Spirit

In addition to confirming the forgiveness of sins, Jesus' resurrection also inaugurates the new life promised in the New Covenant. This new life is marked by the indwelling of the Holy Spirit, who empowers believers to live according to God's will and internalizes the law within their hearts, as promised in Jeremiah 31:33: "I will put my law within them, and I will write it on their hearts."

Jesus' resurrection and ascension led to the outpouring of the Holy Spirit at Pentecost, as recorded in Acts 2. The coming of the Holy Spirit is seen as the fulfillment of the New Covenant's promise of internal transformation. In Romans 8:2-4, Paul explains how the Spirit empowers believers to live out the righteousness of the law:

> "For the law of the Spirit of life has set you free in Christ Jesus from the law of sin and death... in order that the righteous requirement of the law might be fulfilled in us, who walk not according to the flesh but according to the Spirit." (ESV)

Through the resurrection and the gift of the Holy Spirit, believers are enabled to live in the new reality of the New Covenant, where the law is no longer an external code but is written on their hearts.

5. The Ongoing Impact of the New Covenant

The fulfillment of the New Covenant in Jesus' death and resurrection has ongoing implications for Christian life and theology. Believers live in the reality of the New Covenant, enjoying a transformed relationship with God that is characterized by grace, forgiveness, and empowerment through the Holy Spirit.

5.1 Direct Access to God

Under the Old Covenant, access to God was mediated by priests, and only the high priest could enter the Holy of Holies once a year to offer sacrifices for the people's sins. However, the New Covenant, established by Jesus, grants all believers direct access to God. In Hebrews 10:19-22, the writer encourages believers to approach God with confidence:

> "Therefore, brothers, since we have confidence to enter the holy places by the blood of Jesus... let us draw near with a true heart in full assurance of faith." (ESV)

This direct access to God is a hallmark of the New Covenant, where all believers, regardless of their status or background, can have a personal relationship with God.

5.2 The Universal Scope of the New Covenant

While Jeremiah's prophecy was initially addressed to Israel and Judah, Christians believe that the New Covenant extends beyond ethnic Israel to include all nations. Jesus' Great Commission in Matthew 28:19-20 reflects this universal scope:

> "Go therefore and make disciples of all nations, baptizing them in the name of the Father and of the Son and

of the Holy Spirit, teaching them to observe all that I have commanded you." (ESV)

The New Covenant is open to all who believe in Jesus, fulfilling God's promise to bless all the nations of the earth through Abraham's offspring (Genesis 12:3).

6. Conclusion: Jesus as the Mediator and Fulfillment of the New Covenant

Jeremiah's prophecy of a New Covenant is central to Christian theology, and for Christians, Jesus is the ultimate fulfillment of that prophecy. Through His teachings, Jesus emphasized the internalization of God's law and a personal relationship with God. Through His sacrificial death on the cross, He established the New Covenant, offering complete forgiveness of sins. And through His resurrection, He inaugurated new life for all who believe in Him, empowered by the Holy Spirit to live in accordance with God's will.

For Christians, the New Covenant is not just a future promise but a present reality, one that defines their relationship with God and offers the assurance of salvation, forgiveness, and eternal life. In this way, Jesus stands as the mediator and fulfillment of the New Covenant, bringing about the transformation and redemption that Jeremiah prophesied centuries before.

The Law Written on Hearts

1. Introduction: Spiritual Transformation in the New Covenant

In Jeremiah 31:33, the prophet reveals one of the most profound promises of the New Covenant: the transformation of the heart. God declares:

> "I will put my law within them, and I will write it on their hearts. And I will be their God, and they shall be my people." (ESV)

This passage signifies a shift from the Old Covenant's external adherence to the Mosaic Law, inscribed on stone tablets, to an internal transformation that would enable God's people to live in alignment with His will. Instead of merely following regulations, under the New Covenant, God's people would have His law inscribed on their hearts, shaping their desires, values, and actions from within.

For Christians, this promise is fulfilled through the work of Jesus Christ and the indwelling of the Holy Spirit. This chapter will explore the nature of this spiritual transformation, how it contrasts with the limitations of the Old Covenant, and the role of the Holy Spirit in writing God's law on the hearts of believers, empowering them to live in a new relationship with God.

2. The Law of the Old Covenant: External Regulations

To understand the significance of the law being written on hearts, it is essential to grasp how the law functioned under the Old Covenant. The Mosaic Law, given at Mount Sinai, was a set of external regulations meant to govern the moral, ceremonial, and civil life of Israel. It served as a guide for righteousness and was intended to set Israel apart as a holy nation before God.

2.1 The External Nature of the Law

The Mosaic Law was external in nature. It was written on stone tablets and communicated through Moses, dictating how the people should act, worship, and live in community. While the law was perfect in its reflection of God's holiness, it was fundamentally outside of the people. The law showed them what righteousness looked like, but it could not transform their hearts or give them the power to fully live in obedience.

In Deuteronomy 30:10, Moses emphasized the importance of obeying God's commands:

> "When you obey the voice of the LORD your God, to keep his commandments and his statutes that are written in this Book of the Law, when you turn to the LORD your God with all your heart and with all your soul." (ESV)

Despite the call for wholehearted obedience, Israel repeatedly struggled to keep the law. This struggle stemmed from the fact that while the law could instruct behavior, it could not change the inward disposition of the people. As a result, Israel's history under the Old Covenant was marked by cycles of disobedience, repentance, and judgment.

2.2 The Limitations of External Law

The Old Covenant revealed humanity's inability to live up to God's righteous standards. The law was good, but human sinfulness made it impossible to fully comply with its demands. The external nature of the law—written on tablets, carried out through rituals, and enforced through rules—could not address the deeper issue: the sinfulness of the human heart.

In Jeremiah 17:9, the prophet laments the condition of the human heart:

> "The heart is deceitful above all things, and desperately sick; who can understand it?" (ESV)

The law could identify sin but not cure the underlying condition. As Paul explains in Romans 7:7, the law exposed sin: "If it had not been for the law, I would not have known sin." However, the law lacked the power to deliver humanity from sin. This limitation led to the need for a New Covenant, one that would transform people from the inside out, healing the heart and empowering a new kind of obedience.

3. The Promise of a New Covenant: Internal Transformation

In response to Israel's failure to keep the Old Covenant, God promises a New Covenant through the prophet Jeremiah. This New Covenant would be different, for it would address the heart of the problem—human sinfulness—by transforming the heart itself. The key to this transformation is God's promise to write His law on the hearts of His people, signifying a radical internalization of His will.

3.1 The Law Written on Hearts

In Jeremiah 31:33, God makes a profound promise to His people:

> "For this is the covenant that I will make with the house of Israel after those days, declares the LORD: I will put my law within them, and I will write it on their hearts. And I will be their God, and they shall be my people." (ESV)

This promise of internalizing the law is at the heart of the New Covenant. Instead of external rules and regulations, God's law would become an integral part of the believer's heart, mind, and will. This transformation would not merely change behavior but would reshape the person's very identity, inclinations, and desires.

The internalization of the law is transformative in two key ways:

- A New Disposition Toward God's Will: Instead of struggling against an external code, God's people would have a new desire to follow His will. The law written on the heart signifies an alignment of the believer's desires with God's purposes. Obedience would come not from compulsion but from a genuine, inward desire to please God.

- A Restored Relationship with God: God's promise to write His law on the hearts of His people reflects a deeper, more intimate relationship. As Jeremiah proclaims, "I will be their God, and they shall be my people." This covenant relationship is not based on legal adherence but on a transformed heart that delights in God's presence and seeks to live in accordance with His ways.

3.2 Ezekiel's Vision: A New Heart and Spirit

The promise of internal transformation is echoed in the prophecy of Ezekiel, who envisions a time when God will replace the people's stony, disobedient hearts with hearts of flesh—hearts that are responsive to His will. In Ezekiel 36:26-27, God declares:

> "And I will give you a new heart, and a new spirit I will put within you. And I will remove the heart of stone from your flesh and give you a heart of flesh. And I will put my Spirit within you, and cause you to walk in my statutes and be careful to obey my rules." (ESV)

Here, Ezekiel further clarifies how this transformation will take place: through the giving of God's Spirit. The indwelling presence of the Holy Spirit would be the means by which God writes His law on the hearts of His people, enabling them to live in obedience and faithfulness.

4. The Role of the Holy Spirit in the New Covenant

In Christian theology, the promise of the law being written on the heart is fulfilled through the indwelling of the Holy Spirit. The Holy Spirit plays a central role in the New Covenant by enabling believers to live according to God's will, empowering them to experience the spiritual transformation that was impossible under the Old Covenant.

4.1 The Indwelling of the Holy Spirit

One of the defining features of the New Covenant is that the Holy Spirit comes to dwell within believers, making possible the internal transformation promised by Jeremiah and Ezekiel. In John 14:16-17, Jesus speaks of the coming of the Holy Spirit:

> "And I will ask the Father, and he will give you another Helper, to be with you forever, even the Spirit of truth... You know him, for he dwells with you and will be in you." (ESV)

The Holy Spirit's indwelling presence fulfills the promise of the New Covenant, as the Spirit writes God's law on the hearts of believers, guiding them into truth and enabling them to live out God's commandments.

4.2 The Holy Spirit as the Source of Obedience

The Holy Spirit not only convicts believers of sin and brings about repentance but also empowers them to live in obedience to God's will. The internal transformation wrought by the Spirit enables believers to fulfill the righteous requirements of the law, not through their own strength but through the power of the Spirit working within them.

Paul speaks of this transformative power in Romans 8:3-4:

> "For God has done what the law, weakened by the flesh, could not do. By sending his own Son in the likeness of sinful flesh... in order that the righteous requirement of the law might be fulfilled in us, who walk not according to the flesh but according to the Spirit." (ESV)

The Holy Spirit enables believers to "walk according to the Spirit," meaning they live in alignment with God's will, not because they are externally compelled but because their hearts have been changed. The Spirit produces the fruit of righteousness in their lives, reflecting the internalization of God's law.

4.3 The Spirit as the Seal of the New Covenant

In addition to empowering obedience, the Holy Spirit serves as the seal and guarantee of the New Covenant. Paul describes the Holy Spirit as the "guarantee" of believers' inheritance in Christ, signifying their belonging to God and their participation in the New Covenant.

In Ephesians 1:13-14, Paul writes:

> "In him you also, when you heard the word of truth, the gospel of your salvation, and believed in him, were sealed with the promised Holy Spirit, who is the guarantee of our inheritance until we acquire possession of it." (ESV)

The Holy Spirit's presence in the life of the believer is the evidence that they are participants in the New Covenant, experiencing the forgiveness, transformation, and relationship with God that Jeremiah promised.

5. Living Under the New Covenant: The Transformed Heart

For Christians, living under the New Covenant means living in the reality of a transformed heart, empowered by the Holy Spirit to live in accordance with God's will. This transformation is not merely about outward obedience to rules but about an internal, Spirit-led relationship with God that produces a new way of living.

5.1 The Fruit of the Spirit

The evidence of the law written on the heart is seen in the transformation of character that comes through the work of the Holy Spirit. In Galatians 5:22-23, Paul describes the fruit of the Spirit:

> "But the fruit of the Spirit is love, joy, peace, patience, kindness, goodness, faithfulness, gentleness, self-control; against such things there is no law." (ESV)

These virtues are not produced by human effort but by the Spirit's work within the believer, demonstrating the internalization of God's law and the fulfillment of Jeremiah's promise.

5.2 Freedom in Christ

Living under the New Covenant also brings freedom. Unlike the Old Covenant, which required strict adherence to external regulations, the New Covenant offers believers freedom in Christ. This freedom is not a license to sin but a freedom to live in alignment with God's will, empowered by the Spirit.

In 2 Corinthians 3:17, Paul writes:

> "Now the Lord is the Spirit, and where the Spirit of the Lord is, there is freedom." (ESV)

This freedom reflects the New Covenant's emphasis on internal transformation rather than external legalism. Believers are free to live as God's people, guided by the Spirit, with His law written on their hearts.

6. Conclusion: The Law Written on Hearts Through the Holy Spirit

Jeremiah's promise of a New Covenant, where God's law would be written on the hearts of His people, finds its fulfillment in the life, death, and resurrection of Jesus Christ and the indwelling of the Holy Spirit. The Holy Spirit plays a central role in this transformation, enabling believers to live in obedience to God's will, not through external compulsion but through the internal renewal of the heart.

For Christians, the New Covenant represents a new way of relating to God, characterized by intimacy, grace, and empowerment through the Holy Spirit. The law written on the heart signifies the profound spiritual transformation that occurs under the New Covenant, allowing believers to live as God's people, with His presence dwelling within them. This fulfillment of Jeremiah's prophecy marks the beginning of a new era in the relationship between God and humanity, one that is defined by the inner work of the Holy Spirit and the transformative power of God's grace.

CHAPTER 09

THE NATURE OF JESUS IN THE GOSPEL OF JOHN

The Gospel of John opens with a profound declaration about the nature of Jesus Christ, identifying Him as the Word (Logos) who existed from the beginning with God and was, in fact, God Himself. This passage is foundational for understanding the divinity of Jesus and His unique relationship with the Father. John 1:1-18 lays the groundwork for the entire Gospel, presenting Jesus as the eternal Word made flesh, full of grace and truth.

The Eternal Word (John 1:1-2)

"In the beginning was the Word, and the Word was with God, and the Word was God. He was in the beginning with God."

From the very first verse, John establishes the eternal existence of Jesus. Unlike other Gospels that start with Jesus' earthly life, John transcends time, asserting that Jesus, as the Word, existed "in the beginning." This phrase echoes the opening words of Genesis, drawing a parallel between the creation account and the new creation inaugurated through Jesus Christ.

The term "Word" (Logos) is rich with meaning. In Greek philosophy, Logos refers to the principle of reason and order in the universe. In Jewish thought, it represents God's spoken word, through which He created and sustains all things. By identifying Jesus as the Logos, John conveys that Jesus is both the divine reason behind the universe and the active agent of creation.

The assertion that "the Word was with God" emphasizes the intimate relationship between Jesus and the Father. It indicates distinct personhood while affirming unity in essence. The climactic statement, "the Word was God," unequivocally declares the deity of Jesus, leaving no room for interpreting Him merely as a created being or lesser divine figure.

The Creator and Sustainer (John 1:3-5)

"All things were made through Him, and without Him, nothing was made that was made. In Him was life, and the life was the light of men. And the light shines in the darkness, and the darkness did not comprehend it."

John further elaborates on the role of Jesus in creation. As the Logos, Jesus is the conduit through which all things came into being. This underscores His omnipotence and preeminence over creation. Nothing exists apart from His creative will and power.

The statement "In Him was life" signifies that Jesus is the source of all life, both physical and spiritual. The life He gives is not merely biological existence but the fullness of life that reflects God's eternal nature. This life is also "the light of men," symbolizing the revelation of God's truth and presence in the world. The light shines in the darkness, representing the invasion of God's kingdom into a world marred by sin and death. Despite the resistance and inability of darkness to overcome it, the light remains triumphant.

The Witness of John the Baptist (John 1:6-8)

"There was a man sent from God, whose name was John. This man came for a witness, to bear witness of the Light, that all through him might believe. He was not that Light, but was sent to bear witness of that Light."

John the Baptist plays a crucial role in the narrative, serving as the forerunner who prepares the way for Jesus. His mission is to testify about the Light, pointing people to Jesus so that they might believe. John the Baptist's role highlights the importance of testimony in God's redemptive plan. His witness validates Jesus' identity and mission, affirming that He is the true Light sent to illuminate every person.

The Rejection and Reception of the Word (John 1:9-13)

"That was the true Light which gives light to every man coming into the world. He was in the world, and the world was made through Him, and the world did not know Him. He came to His own, and His own did not receive Him. But as many as received Him, to them He gave the right to become children of God, to those who believe in His name: who were born, not of blood, nor of the will of the flesh, nor of the will of man, but of God."

Jesus, as the true Light, came into the world He created, yet He was not recognized or received by it. This rejection is particularly poignant among His own people, the Jews, who were awaiting the Messiah. Their failure to recognize Him underscores the tragic reality of spiritual blindness and the pervasive influence of sin.

However, John offers a message of hope: those who receive Jesus and believe in His name are given the right to become children of God. This new birth is not based on a natural descent, human effort, or decision but is a divine act of grace. It highlights the transformative power of faith in Jesus, enabling believers to enter into a familial relationship with God.

The Word Became Flesh (John 1:14)

"And the Word became flesh and dwelt among us, and we beheld His glory, the glory as of the only begotten of the Father, full of grace and truth."

The incarnation is the pinnacle of the prologue's revelation. The eternal Word took on human flesh, entering the realm of human experience and existence. This profound mystery—God becoming man—demonstrates God's immense love and commitment to redeeming humanity.

The phrase "dwelt among us" evokes the imagery of the Tabernacle in the Old Testament, where God's presence resided among His people. Jesus is the ultimate fulfillment of this concept, embodying God's presence in a tangible and accessible way.

John testifies to witnessing Jesus' glory, a glory that reflects His unique relationship with the Father as the only begotten Son. This glory is characterized by grace and truth, qualities that define Jesus' ministry and reveal the nature of God. Grace emphasizes God's unmerited favor and love, while truth underscores His faithfulness and reliability.

The Testimony of John the Baptist (John 1:15)

"John bore witness of Him and cried out, saying, 'This was He of whom I said, "He who comes after me is preferred before me, for He was before me."'"

John the Baptist reaffirms Jesus' preeminence and eternal existence. Despite coming after John in terms of earthly ministry, Jesus surpasses him because He existed before him. This statement reinforces the divine nature of Jesus and His superiority over all human prophets and messengers.

Grace and Truth Through Jesus Christ (John 1:16-18)

"And of His fullness, we have all received, and grace for grace. For the law was given through Moses, but grace and truth came through Jesus Christ. No one has seen God at any time. The only begotten Son, who is in the bosom of the Father, He has declared Him."

In Jesus, believers receive the fullness of God's grace, continually renewed and overflowing. This grace contrasts with the law given through Moses, which, while revealing God's standards, could not provide the means for true redemption and transformation. Jesus embodies and imparts both grace and truth, offering salvation and revealing the true nature of God.

John concludes by affirming that Jesus, the only begotten Son, is uniquely qualified to reveal God to humanity. No one has seen God, but Jesus, who is intimately united with the Father, makes Him known. This declaration confirms that knowing Jesus is the key to knowing God.

Conclusion

The opening chapter of the Gospel of John presents a profound theological exposition of Jesus' divinity. It asserts His eternal existence, creative power, and unique role as the incarnate Word. Through His life, teachings, and sacrificial death, Jesus reveals the fullness of God's grace and truth, inviting all who believe in Him to become children of God. This foundational understanding of Jesus as the divine Word sets the stage for the rest of the Gospel, which continually unveils His divine identity and redemptive mission.

All Things Were Made Through Him

In the opening verses of the Gospel of John, a profound truth is revealed: "All things were made through Him; and without Him, nothing was made that was made" (John 1:3). This verse is pivotal in understanding the divine nature of Jesus Christ. It highlights His role as the Creator and Sustainer of the universe, affirming His deity and preeminence over all creation. This chapter will delve into the implications of this verse, exploring how it underscores Jesus' divine nature and His integral role in the cosmos.

The Preeminence of Christ in Creation

"All things were made through Him..."

John 1:3 declares that all things were made through Jesus, indicating that He is the agent of creation. This statement places Jesus at the very heart of the creative process, affirming that He is not a mere participant but the divine source through whom everything came into existence. This echoes the creation account in Genesis, where God's spoken word brings the universe into being. By identifying Jesus as the Logos (Word), John asserts that Jesus is the divine Word spoken at creation.

In Colossians 1:16, the Apostle Paul reinforces this truth: "For by Him all things were created that are in heaven and that are on earth, visible and invisible, whether thrones or dominions or principalities or powers. All things were created through Him and for Him." This verse expands on John's declaration, emphasizing that Jesus is the Creator of everything, both seen and unseen. His creative power extends to the entire cosmos, from the smallest atom to the vast galaxies, as well as spiritual realms and authorities.

The Sustainer of All Things

"...without Him, nothing was made that was made."

The latter part of John 1:3 underscores the absolute dependence of all creation on Jesus. Without Him, nothing was made that exists. This statement affirms that Jesus is not only the Creator but also the Sustainer of all things. Everything owes its existence to Him, and nothing can exist apart from His sustaining power.

Hebrews 1:3 speaks to this sustaining role: "Who being the brightness of His glory and the express image of His person, and upholding all things by the word of His power, when He had by Himself purged our sins, sat down at the right hand of the Majesty on high." Jesus upholds the universe by His powerful word, maintaining the order and function of all creation. This continuous act of sustaining the universe is a testament to His divine nature and authority.

The Divine Nature of Jesus

The Eternal Word

The concept of Jesus as the Logos, or Word, is central to understanding His divine nature. In Greek philosophy, Logos signifies the rational principle that governs the universe. In Jewish thought, it represents God's active word in creation and revelation. By identifying Jesus as the Logos, John bridges these concepts, presenting Jesus as the divine reason and the agent through whom God created and sustains the world.

John 1:1-2 establishes Jesus' eternal nature: "In the beginning was the Word, and the Word was with God, and the Word was God. He was in the beginning with God." These verses affirm that Jesus existed before creation, co-eternal with God the Father. He is not a created being but the eternal Word who has always been with God and is Himself, God. This eternal existence is a hallmark of His divine nature, distinguishing Him from all created beings.

The Incarnation: The Word Became Flesh

John 1:14

The divine nature of Jesus is further revealed in the incarnation: "And the Word became flesh and dwelt among us, and we beheld His glory, the glory as of the only begotten of the Father, full of grace and truth." The eternal Word took on human flesh, entering the realm of human experience. This profound mystery—God becoming man—demonstrates the fullness of Jesus' divine nature.

The incarnation does not diminish Jesus' divinity; rather, it reveals the depth of God's love and His commitment to redeeming humanity. Jesus, fully God and fully man, bridges the gap between the divine and human, providing a way for humanity to be reconciled with God. This dual nature of Jesus—His divinity and humanity—is central to Christian theology and the understanding of His role as Savior.

Jesus is the Image of the Invisible God

Colossians 1:15 describes Jesus as "the image of the invisible God, the firstborn over all creation." As the image of God, Jesus perfectly reveals the nature and character of God the Father. He is the visible representation of the invisible God, making God's attributes and will known to humanity. This revelation is part of His divine nature, as only God can fully reveal Himself.

The term "firstborn over all creation" does not imply that Jesus is a created being but signifies His preeminence and authority over all creation. In Jewish culture, the firstborn held a position of honor and authority. By calling

Jesus the firstborn, Paul emphasizes His supreme status and His rightful place as Lord over all creation.

The Implications of Jesus' Divine Nature

Worship and Obedience

Recognizing Jesus as the Creator and Sustainer of all things calls for worship and obedience. His divine nature demands reverence and submission. As the one through whom all things were made, Jesus is worthy of all honor and praise. Revelation 4:11 captures this truth: "You are worthy, O Lord, to receive glory and honor and power; for You created all things, and by Your will they exist and were created."

Assurance of Salvation

Jesus' divine nature also assures believers of the efficacy of His redemptive work. As fully God, Jesus' sacrifice on the cross is of infinite value, sufficient to atone for the sins of the whole world. His resurrection demonstrates His power over death and guarantees eternal life for those who believe in Him. This assurance is rooted in His divine authority and power.

Conclusion

John 1:3 reveals the profound truth of Jesus' divine nature as the Creator and Sustainer of all things. Through Him, everything came into existence, and without Him, nothing exists. This foundational understanding of Jesus' divinity shapes our perception of His role in the cosmos and His redemptive mission. As the eternal Word, Jesus bridges the gap between the divine and human, revealing God's nature and providing a way for reconciliation. His divine nature calls us to worship, obedience, and assurance in His redemptive work. In recognizing Jesus as the Creator and Sustainer, we acknowledge His supreme authority and honor Him as the eternal Word made flesh.

In Him Was Life, and the Life Was the Light of Men

The opening chapter of the Gospel of John is rich with profound theological insights about the divine nature of Jesus Christ. John 1:4-5 states, "In Him was life, and the life was the light of men. And the light shines in the darkness, and the darkness did not comprehend it." This passage encapsulates the essence of Jesus' divinity by portraying Him as the source of life and light for humanity. In this chapter, we will delve into the deep implications of these verses, exploring how they reveal Jesus' divine nature and His role in bringing life and light to the world.

Jesus as the Source of Life

"In Him was life..."

The declaration that "In Him was life" emphasizes that Jesus is the ultimate source of all life. This statement is foundational for understanding His divine nature. Life, in this context, is not merely biological existence but encompasses spiritual and eternal life. It signifies the fullness of life that only God can give.

In the Old Testament, God is often depicted as the source of life. For instance, Psalm 36:9 states, "For with You is the fountain of life; in Your light we see light." By attributing life to Jesus, John aligns Him with the divine identity of God, underscoring His deity. Jesus Himself confirms this in John 14:6, where He declares, "I am the way, the truth, and the life. No one comes to the Father except through Me." This assertion not only highlights His unique role in salvation but also affirms His inherent life-giving power.

The Life-Giver in Creation and Redemption

Jesus' role as the source of life is evident in both creation and redemption. In the creation narrative, God's breath brings life to humanity (Genesis 2:7). Similarly, John 1:3-4 reveals that all creation came into being through Jesus, who imparts life to all living things. This creative power is a hallmark of His divine nature.

In the realm of redemption, Jesus' life-giving power is manifested through His death and resurrection. In John 10:10, Jesus states, "I have come that they may have life, and that they may have it more abundantly." Through His sacrificial death on the cross and His victorious resurrection, Jesus conquers sin and death, offering eternal life to all who believe in Him. This redemptive work is the ultimate expression of His divine nature and His love for humanity.

Jesus as the Light of Men

"...and the life was the light of men."

The second part of John 1:4, "and the life was the light of men," further elaborates on Jesus' divine nature. Light, in biblical symbolism, often represents truth, holiness, and the revelation of God's presence. By describing Jesus as the light of men, John emphasizes that Jesus is the source of divine illumination, guiding humanity out of spiritual darkness and into the truth of God's kingdom.

The Light in Creation and Revelation

The concept of light is deeply rooted in the biblical narrative. In Genesis 1:3, God's first creative act is to speak light into existence: "Then God said, 'Let there be light'; and there was light." This primordial light is a symbol of God's presence and the order He brings to chaos. By identifying Jesus as the light, John connects Him to this creative and revelatory act of God, affirming His divine authority and purpose.

In John 8:12, Jesus proclaims, "I am the light of the world. He who follows Me shall not walk in darkness but have the light of life." This statement highlights Jesus' role in revealing God's truth and dispelling the darkness of sin and ignorance. His teachings, miracles, and very presence embody the light of divine revelation, making God's nature and will known to humanity.

The Light Shines in the Darkness

"And the light shines in the darkness, and the darkness did not comprehend it."

John 1:5 introduces a powerful metaphor of light shining in the darkness. This imagery conveys the ongoing struggle between good and evil, truth and falsehood, life and death. The darkness represents the sinful, fallen state of the world, as opposed to the light of God's truth and holiness.

The Inextinguishable Light

The phrase "the light shines in the darkness" is in the present tense, indicating a continuous action. It signifies that Jesus' light persistently illuminates the darkness, offering hope and redemption. The subsequent statement, "and the darkness did not comprehend it," can also be translated as "the darkness did not overcome it." This dual meaning underscores both the ignorance of the world in recognizing Jesus and the ultimate triumph of His light over darkness.

This victory of light over darkness is a central theme in John's Gospel. Jesus' crucifixion, seemingly a moment of darkness, culminates in the resurrection, the ultimate demonstration of light overcoming darkness. This triumph is a testament to Jesus' divine power and His mission to bring salvation to the world.

The Divine Nature of Jesus as Light and Life

The Self-Existence of Jesus

The declarations that Jesus is the source of life and the light of men reveal His self-existence, a key attribute of divinity. Unlike created beings who derive their life from external sources, Jesus possesses life inherently. This self-existence is an essential characteristic of God, as seen in Exodus 3:14, where God reveals Himself to Moses as "I AM WHO I AM." By ascribing life and light to Jesus, John affirms His co-equality with God the Father.

The Transformative Power of Jesus

Jesus' divine nature as the source of life and light has profound implications for believers. As the life-giver, Jesus offers not only physical existence but also spiritual renewal and eternal life. Believers are called to experience this abundant life through faith in Him. As the light of men, Jesus illuminates the path to righteousness, guiding believers in truth and revealing God's will.

The transformative power of Jesus is evident in the lives of those who follow Him. In 2 Corinthians 5:17, Paul writes, "Therefore, if anyone is in Christ, he is a new creation; old things have passed away; behold, all things have become new." This new creation is a result of the life and light that Jesus imparts, bringing believers into a restored relationship with God.

Conclusion

John 1:4-5 encapsulates the divine nature of Jesus by presenting Him as the source of life and the light of men. These verses reveal that Jesus is not merely a historical figure or a moral teacher but the eternal Word who imparts life and illuminates the truth of God. His life-giving power and His role as the light of the world affirm His deity and His mission to redeem humanity.

As the light shines in the darkness and the darkness cannot overcome it, believers are called to embrace the life and light that Jesus offers. This call invites a transformative relationship with Him, one that brings eternal life and the revelation of God's truth. In recognizing Jesus as the divine source of life and light, we are drawn into a deeper understanding of His nature and His redemptive work, leading us to worship, follow, and share His light with the world.

The Word Became Flesh and Dwelt Among Us

John 1:14 is one of the most profound verses in the Bible, encapsulating the mystery and majesty of the incarnation: "The Word became flesh and dwelt among us, full of grace and truth." This verse is central to understanding the divine nature of Jesus Christ, as it reveals how the eternal Word, who is God, took on human flesh and lived among humanity. In this chapter, we will explore the implications of this verse, delving into the significance of the Word becoming flesh and the manifestation of grace and truth in Jesus.

The Word Became Flesh

The Eternal Word

The opening of John's Gospel introduces Jesus as the Word (Logos), establishing His preexistence and divine nature: "In the beginning was the Word, and the Word was with God, and the Word was God" (John 1:1). The term Logos was rich with meaning in both Greek philosophy and Jewish thought, symbolizing divine reason, order, and creative power. By identifying Jesus as the Logos, John asserts that Jesus is both the agent of creation and the ultimate revelation of God.

The Incarnation

"The Word became flesh" is a declaration of the incarnation, the momentous event where the eternal, divine Word took on human nature. This act of becoming flesh signifies that Jesus, while remaining fully God, also became fully human. The incarnation is a unique and unparalleled event in the history of the world, where God entered into the human experience.

The Apostle Paul echoes this mystery in Philippians 2:6-7: "Who, being in the form of God, did not consider it robbery to be equal with God, but made Himself of no reputation, taking the form of a bondservant, and coming in the likeness of men." Jesus, though equal to God, humbled Himself by becoming a man, demonstrating the depth of His love and the extent of His willingness to redeem humanity.

Dwelt Among Us

God With Us

The phrase "dwelt among us" translates into a Greek term that literally means "pitched His tent" or "tabernacled" among us. This imagery is significant, as it recalls the Old Testament Tabernacle where God's presence dwelled among the Israelites during their journey through the wilderness. In the same way, Jesus, the Word made flesh, is the ultimate fulfillment of God's desire to dwell among His people.

The concept of God dwelling among His people is a recurring theme in Scripture. In the Old Testament, God's presence was manifest in the Tabernacle and later in the temple. However, these were mere shadows of the ultimate reality fulfilled in Jesus. As Emmanuel, "God with us" (Matthew 1:23), Jesus embodies God's presence in a direct and personal way. Through Him, humanity can encounter

God not as a distant deity but as a loving and accessible Savior.

The Glory of God Revealed

John continues, "And we beheld His glory, the glory as of the only begotten of the Father." The incarnation allows us to see the glory of God in the person of Jesus Christ. This glory is not merely a radiant display but the manifestation of God's character and nature. Jesus' life, teachings, miracles, death, and resurrection all reveal the divine glory.

In the Old Testament, Moses asked to see God's glory, and God responded that no one could see His face and live (Exodus 33:18-20). Yet, in Jesus, the fullness of God's glory is revealed in a way that humanity can behold. As the only begotten Son, Jesus uniquely reflects the Father's glory, providing a clear and tangible revelation of God's character.

Full of Grace and Truth

The Grace of God

Jesus is described as being "full of grace." Grace is the unmerited favor of God, His love and kindness extended to undeserving humanity. Throughout His ministry, Jesus exemplified grace in His interactions with people. He showed compassion to the sick, the sinner, and the outcast, offering forgiveness and healing without condition.

One of the most poignant examples of Jesus' grace is His encounter with the woman caught in adultery (John 8:1-11). Despite the legalistic demands for her punishment, Jesus extends grace, saying, "Neither do I condemn you; go and sin no more." This act of grace not only forgives her sin but empowers her to live a transformed life.

The ultimate expression of Jesus' grace is seen in His sacrificial death on the cross. Paul writes in Ephesians 2:8-

9, "For by grace you have been saved through faith, and that not of yourselves; it is the gift of God, not of works, lest anyone should boast." Jesus' grace provides the way of salvation, reconciling humanity to God and offering eternal life.

The Truth of God

Jesus is also described as being "full of truth." In a world marred by deception and falsehood, Jesus embodies the absolute truth of God. He declares in John 14:6, "I am the way, the truth, and the life. No one comes to the Father except through Me." This claim to be the truth is exclusive and definitive, affirming that a true understanding of God and His will can only be found in Jesus.

Throughout His ministry, Jesus taught the truth about God's kingdom, correcting misconceptions and revealing the deeper realities of God's purposes. His teachings, such as the Sermon on the Mount, provide profound insights into the nature of God's righteousness and the ethical demands of His kingdom.

Moreover, Jesus' life was a living testimony to the truth. He lived a sinless life, perfectly embodying God's commandments and demonstrating the truth of God's love and holiness. His resurrection from the dead is the ultimate vindication of His truth claims, proving His divine authority and the truth of His message.

The Intersection of Grace and Truth

In Jesus, grace and truth are perfectly united. This balance is essential for understanding His divine nature and mission. Grace without truth can lead to permissiveness and a disregard for God's holiness, while truth without grace can result in legalism and condemnation. Jesus embodies both, offering grace that transforms and truth that liberates.

John 1:16-17 further emphasizes this: "And of His fullness we have all received, and grace for grace. For the law was given through Moses, but grace and truth came through Jesus Christ." The law, given through Moses, revealed God's standards but also highlighted humanity's inability to meet them. Jesus, however, brings the fullness of God's grace and truth, providing the means for salvation and the revelation of God's true nature.

The Divine Nature of Jesus in the Incarnation

The Humility of God

The incarnation reveals the profound humility of God. In Philippians 2:8, Paul writes, "And being found in appearance as a man, He humbled Himself and became obedient to the point of death, even the death of the cross." Jesus' willingness to become human and endure suffering and death demonstrates the depth of God's love and His commitment to redeeming humanity.

This humility is also seen in Jesus' life of service. In John 13:1-17, Jesus washes His disciples' feet, an act of humility and service that exemplifies His teachings about greatness in God's kingdom. Through His actions, Jesus reveals that true greatness is found in serving others, reflecting the self-giving love of God.

The Revelation of God

The incarnation also reveals God's desire to be known by His creation. Throughout history, God has communicated with humanity through various means, including prophets, scriptures, and divine interventions. In Jesus, however, God provides the ultimate revelation of Himself. Hebrews 1:1-2 states, "God, who at various times and in various ways spoke in time past to the fathers by the prophets, has in these last days spoken to us by His Son."

Jesus' life and teachings are the clearest and most direct revelation of God's character, will, and purposes. Through Him, we see the fullness of God's grace and truth, His love and justice, His mercy and holiness. This revelation invites us into a personal relationship with God, grounded in the knowledge of who He is as revealed in Jesus Christ.

Conclusion

John 1:14 encapsulates the mystery and majesty of the incarnation, revealing the divine nature of Jesus Christ. The eternal Word becoming flesh and dwelling among us is the ultimate expression of God's love and His desire to redeem and restore humanity. In Jesus, we behold the glory of God, full of grace and truth, inviting us to experience His life-transforming power.

As we contemplate the profound truths of this verse, we are drawn into a deeper understanding of who Jesus is and what He has accomplished. His incarnation calls us to worship, follow, and share the good news of His grace and truth with the world. Through Him, we encounter the fullness of God's love and the revelation of His divine nature, leading us into a life of faith, hope, and eternal fellowship with God.

No One Has Ever Seen God

John 1:18 (NIV) states, "No one has ever seen God, but the one and only Son, who is himself God and is in closest relationship with the Father, has made him known." This verse is profound in its declaration of Jesus' divine nature and His unique role in revealing God to humanity. It encapsulates the mystery of the incarnation and the intimate relationship between the Father and the Son. In this chapter, we will delve into the implications of this verse, exploring how it reveals Jesus' divine nature and His mission to make God known.

The Invisibility of God

"No one has ever seen God..."

The assertion that no one has ever seen God highlights the fundamental truth about God's nature: His invisibility and transcendence. Throughout the Old Testament, God is depicted as dwelling in unapproachable light, unseen by human eyes. Exodus 33:20 states, "But," he said, "you cannot see my face, for no one may see me and live." This emphasizes the holiness and majesty of God, who is beyond the capacity of human perception.

The invisibility of God underscores the need for a mediator, someone who can bridge the gap between the divine and human. This sets the stage for the revelation of Jesus Christ, the one who makes the invisible God known to humanity.

The Unique Revelation of the Son

"...but the one and only Son, who is himself God and is in closest relationship with the Father..."

This part of the verse introduces the unique status of Jesus as the "one and only Son," affirming His deity and His intimate relationship with the Father. The phrase "who is himself God" leaves no ambiguity about Jesus' divine nature. He is not merely a prophet or a teacher but God incarnate.

The term "one and only" (Greek: monogenes) signifies Jesus' unique and singular nature. He is the only Son of God in a way that no other being is. This uniqueness is further emphasized by His relationship with the Father, described as "in closest relationship with the Father" (Greek: eis ton kolpon tou Patros), literally meaning "in the bosom of the Father." This imagery conveys an intimate and eternal bond between the Father and the Son, highlighting their unity and mutual love.

Making God Known

"...has made him known."

The climax of the verse is the declaration that Jesus "has made him known." The Greek word used here, exegesato, from which we get the word "exegesis," means to explain, interpret, or reveal. Jesus, as the divine Son, interprets and reveals the Father to humanity. He is the ultimate revelation of God, making the invisible God visible and accessible.

The Role of Jesus in Revelation

The Incarnation as Revelation

The incarnation is the definitive act of revelation. When "the Word became flesh" (John 1:14), God's nature and character were fully revealed in Jesus Christ. Through His life, teachings, miracles, death, and resurrection, Jesus provides a clear and comprehensive picture of who God is. Hebrews 1:3 states, "The Son is the radiance of God's glory and the exact representation of his being, sustaining all things by his powerful word." This affirms that Jesus perfectly reflects God's glory and nature, making Him the ultimate revelation of God.

The Teachings of Jesus

Throughout His ministry, Jesus consistently pointed to His unique relationship with the Father and His role in revealing Him. In John 14:9, Jesus says to Philip, "Anyone who has seen me has seen the Father." This bold statement underscores that to know Jesus is to know God. His teachings about God's kingdom, love, justice, and mercy are direct revelations of the Father's heart and will.

The Miracles of Jesus

The miracles performed by Jesus also serve as a revelation of God's nature. They demonstrate His power, compassion, and authority. For instance, when Jesus heals the sick, raises the dead, and forgives sins, He reveals God's desire for restoration and wholeness. These acts are not just displays of power but signs pointing to the reality of God's kingdom breaking into the world.

The Divine Nature of Jesus

Unity with the Father

The close relationship between Jesus and the Father is central to understanding His divine nature. In John 10:30, Jesus declares, "I and the Father are one." This unity is not merely a unity of purpose but of essence. Jesus shares in the very nature of God, making Him fully divine. This unity is foundational to His ability to reveal God perfectly.

Preexistence and Eternity

The preexistence of Jesus is another key aspect of His divine nature. John 1:1-2 states, "In the beginning was the Word, and the Word was with God, and the Word was God. He was with God in the beginning." Jesus exists from eternity, co-equal and co-eternal with the Father. This eternal existence distinguishes Him from all created beings and affirms His deity.

The Role of the Holy Spirit

The Holy Spirit also plays a vital role in the revelation of Jesus and, consequently, the revelation of the Father. Jesus promises the coming of the Spirit who will guide believers into all truth (John 16:13). The Spirit continues the work of revelation, helping believers understand and experience the fullness of God's nature as revealed in Jesus Christ.

The Implications for Believers

Knowing God Through Jesus

The revelation of God through Jesus has profound implications for believers. It means that the true knowledge of God is found in a personal relationship with Jesus Christ. Through Him, we have access to the Father and can experience His love, grace, and truth. This relationship is the foundation of the Christian faith, providing the assurance of salvation and the hope of eternal life.

The Call to Reflect God's Nature

As followers of Jesus, believers are called to reflect God's nature as revealed in Christ. This involves living lives marked by grace and truth, embodying the love and holiness of God in our interactions with others. The revelation of God in Jesus is not only a theological truth to be affirmed but a transformative reality to be lived out in daily life.

Conclusion

John 1:18 (NIV) encapsulates the profound mystery and majesty of Jesus' divine nature and His unique role in revealing God to humanity. As the one and only Son who is Himself God and in closest relationship with the Father, Jesus makes the invisible God known. Through His incarnation, teachings, miracles, and the ongoing work of the Holy Spirit, Jesus provides the ultimate revelation of God's character and will.

Understanding Jesus as the full revelation of God invites us into a deeper relationship with Him, transforming our lives and calling us to reflect His grace and truth in the world. In knowing Jesus, we come to know the Father, experiencing the fullness of His love and the power of His redemptive work. This foundational truth is at the heart of the Christian faith, shaping our understanding of God and our identity as His children.

Jesus is the Bridge Between Heaven and Earth

The concept of Jesus as the bridge between heaven and earth is beautifully encapsulated in John 1:51. This imagery not only highlights Jesus' unique role as the mediator between God and humanity but also reflects the fulfillment of various Old Testament symbols and prophecies. This chapter explores the significance of Jesus as the bridge, focusing on John 1:51, and delves into how this understanding enriches our comprehension of His divine mission.

Jesus' Declaration in John 1:51

John 1:51 (NIV): "He then added, 'Very truly I tell you, you will see heaven open, and the angels of God ascending and descending on the Son of Man.'"

Context and Analysis

1. Context: Jesus speaks these words to Nathanael, one of His early disciples, who is amazed by Jesus' supernatural knowledge about him.

2. Angels Ascending and Descending: This imagery recalls Jacob's dream in Genesis 28:12, where he saw a ladder reaching to heaven with angels ascending and descending on it.

3. Son of Man: Jesus uses the title "Son of Man," which emphasizes His role as the Messiah and His connection to humanity.

Strong's Concordance Insights:

- Ascending (ἀναβαίνω, anabaino, Strong's G305): To go up, ascend.

- Descending (καταβαίνω, katabaino, Strong's G2597): To come down, descend.

- Son of Man (ὁ υἱὸς τοῦ ἀνθρώπου, ho huios tou anthrōpou, Strong's G5207 and G444): A title Jesus used for Himself, emphasizing His humanity and messianic role.

The Significance of Jesus as the Bridge

1. Mediator Between God and Humanity:

1 Timothy 2:5 (NIV): "For there is one God and one mediator between God and mankind, the man Christ Jesus."

- Explanation: Jesus is the sole mediator who bridges the gap between a holy God and sinful humanity. His life, death, and resurrection enable direct access to God.

2. Fulfillment of Jacob's Ladder:

Genesis 28:12 (NIV): "He had a dream in which he saw a stairway resting on the earth, with its top reaching to heaven, and the angels of God were ascending and descending on it."

- Explanation: Jacob's ladder symbolizes the connection between heaven and earth. Jesus fulfills this vision, becoming the ultimate means of connection between God and humanity.

3. Access to God's Presence:

Ephesians 2:18 (NIV): "For through him we both have access to the Father by one Spirit."

- Explanation: Jesus provides believers with direct access to the Father, breaking down the barriers that separated humanity from God.

4. The Revelation of God's Glory:

John 1:14 (NIV): "The Word became flesh and made his dwelling among us. We have seen his glory, the glory of the one and only Son, who came from the Father, full of grace and truth."

- Explanation: Jesus, as the Word made flesh, reveals God's glory and brings divine grace and truth to humanity.

Theological Implications

1. Incarnation and Revelation:

- Incarnation: Jesus, as God incarnate, embodies the divine presence on earth. He is the tangible manifestation of God's glory and love.

- Revelation: Through Jesus, God reveals His character, will, and redemptive plan.

2. Redemption and Reconciliation:

- Redemption: Jesus' sacrificial death redeems humanity from sin, fulfilling the requirements of divine justice.

- Reconciliation: Through Jesus, humanity is reconciled to God, restoring the broken relationship caused by sin.

2 Corinthians 5:18-19 (NIV):

18 All this is from God, who reconciled us to himself through Christ and gave us the ministry of reconciliation:

19 that God was reconciling the world to himself in Christ, not counting people's sins against them. And he has committed to us the message of reconciliation.

- Explanation: Jesus' work of reconciliation brings peace between God and humanity, allowing believers to become ambassadors of this reconciliation.

3. New Covenant:

- Explanation: Jesus establishes a new covenant through His blood, providing a direct and permanent relationship with God.

Luke 22:20 (NIV): "In the same way, after the supper he took the cup, saying, 'This cup is the new covenant in my blood, which is poured out for you.'"

- Explanation: The new covenant is characterized by grace and truth, fulfilled in Jesus' sacrificial act.

Jesus as the Fulfillment of Old Testament Types

1. The Tabernacle and Temple:

- Explanation: Jesus fulfills the function of the Tabernacle and Temple as the dwelling place of God's presence among His people.

John 2:19-21 (NIV):

19 Jesus answered them, "Destroy this temple, and I will raise it again in three days."

20 They replied, "It has taken forty-six years to build this temple, and you are going to raise it in three days?"

21 But the temple he had spoken of was his body.

- Explanation: Jesus' body is the true temple where God's presence dwells and His resurrection signifies the new, eternal temple.

2. The Sacrificial System:

- Explanation: Jesus is the ultimate sacrifice, fulfilling the Old Testament sacrificial system and providing a once-for-all atonement for sin.

Hebrews 10:10 (NIV): "And by that will, we have been made holy through the sacrifice of the body of Jesus Christ once and for all."

- Explanation: Jesus' sacrifice is sufficient to cleanse from sin and bring believers into a holy relationship with God.

3. The High Priest:

- Explanation: Jesus serves as the eternal High Priest, mediating between God and humanity.

Hebrews 4:14-16 (NIV):

14 Therefore, since we have a great high priest who has ascended into heaven, Jesus the Son of God, let us hold firmly to the faith we profess.

15 For we do not have a high priest who is unable to feel sympathy for our weaknesses, but we have one who has been tempted in every way, just as we are—yet he did not sin.

16 Let us then approach God's throne of grace with confidence, so that we may receive mercy and find grace to help us in our time of need.

- Explanation: Jesus' priestly role assures believers of access to God's grace and mercy.

Practical Implications for Believers

1. Assurance of Salvation:

- Explanation: Believers can have confidence in their salvation, knowing that Jesus has secured their relationship with God.

John 10:28-29 (NIV):

28 I give them eternal life, and they shall never perish; no one will snatch them out of my hand.

29 My Father, who has given them to me, is greater than all; no one can snatch them out of my Father's hand.

- Explanation: Jesus' role as the bridge guarantees eternal security for believers.

2. Empowered Prayer Life:

- Explanation: Believers have direct access to God through Jesus, empowering their prayer life.

Hebrews 4:16 (NIV): "Let us then approach God's throne of grace with confidence, so that we may receive mercy and find grace to help us in our time of need."

- Explanation: The confidence to approach God in prayer is grounded in Jesus' mediating work.

3. Mission and Evangelism:

- Explanation: Believers are called to share the message of reconciliation with others, extending the invitation to experience God's grace.

2 Corinthians 5:20 (NIV): "We are therefore Christ's ambassadors, as though God were making his appeal through us. We implore you on Christ's behalf: Be reconciled to God."

- Explanation: As ambassadors of Christ, believers participate in God's mission to reconcile the world to Himself.

Conclusion

Jesus as the bridge between heaven and earth is a profound theological truth that reveals His unique role in God's redemptive plan. Through His life, death, and resurrection, Jesus provides the way for humanity to be reconciled to God, fulfilling the symbolism of Jacob's ladder and numerous Old Testament types. This understanding enriches our comprehension of Jesus' divine mission and its practical implications for believers, offering assurance of salvation, empowering prayer, and motivating mission. By recognizing Jesus as the ultimate mediator, we gain a deeper appreciation of His sacrifice and the access to God's presence that He provides.

CHAPTER 10

JESUS AS THE LIGHT OF THE WORLD

In the Gospel of John, Jesus is portrayed as the true light that gives light to every person coming into the world. John 1:9-13 (NIV) states, "The true light that gives light to everyone was coming into the world. He was in the world, and though the world was made through him, the world did not recognize him. He came to that which was his own, but his own did not receive him. Yet to all who did receive him, to those who believed in his name, he gave the right to become children of God—children born not of natural descent, nor of human decision or a husband's will, but born of God." This chapter delves into the implications of these verses, exploring how they reveal the divine nature of Jesus and His role as the light of the world.

The True Light

"The true light that gives light to everyone was coming into the dworld."

The declaration that Jesus is the "true light" highlights His unique and unparalleled role in illuminating the spiritual darkness of the world. Light, in biblical symbolism, often represents truth, purity, and the presence of God. By calling Jesus the true light, John affirms that Jesus is the ultimate source of divine truth and revelation.

Throughout the Bible, light is associated with God and His guidance. In the Old Testament, God's word is described as a lamp to guide the way (Psalm 119:105). In the New Testament, Jesus embodies this divine light, bringing clarity, direction, and hope to a world darkened by sin and ignorance. His coming into the world signifies the dawn of a new era where God's truth is fully revealed through Him.

The Rejection of the Light

"He was in the world, and though the world was made through him, the world did not recognize him. He came to that which was his own, but his own did not receive him."

These verses poignantly describe the tragedy of humanity's response to Jesus. Despite being the Creator of the world, Jesus was not recognized by the world He made. This failure to recognize Him underscores the spiritual blindness and hardness of the heart that pervades humanity.

Jesus' rejection by His own people, the Israelites, is particularly tragic. As the chosen people of God, they had been prepared through the law and the prophets to recognize the Messiah. Yet, when the true light came, they did not receive Him. This rejection fulfills the prophecy of Isaiah 53:3, which describes the suffering servant as "despised and rejected by mankind."

The Acceptance of the Light

"Yet to all who did receive him, to those who believed in his name, he gave the right to become children of God."

Despite widespread rejection, there is a profound promise for those who receive and believe in Jesus. To these individuals, Jesus gives them the right to become children of God. This right is not based on natural descent, human decision, or a husband's will, but is a divine gift of grace.

The Divine Nature of Jesus as the Light

The Source of Divine Illumination

Jesus' role as the light of the world underscores His divine nature as the source of all spiritual illumination. In John 8:12, Jesus declares, "I am the light of the world. Whoever follows me will never walk in darkness, but will have the light of life." This statement affirms that Jesus is not only the revealer of God's truth but also the sustainer of spiritual life.

Throughout His ministry, Jesus illuminated the truth of God's kingdom, corrected misconceptions, and revealed the heart of God. His teachings, such as the Sermon on the Mount, provide profound insights into the nature of God's righteousness and the ethical demands of His kingdom. Jesus' miracles also serve as signs of His divine light, demonstrating His power over darkness, disease, and death.

The Revelation of God

As the true light, Jesus reveals the nature and character of God. In John 14:9, He tells Philip, "Anyone who has seen me has seen the Father." This declaration affirms that Jesus is the visible representation of the invisible God. Through His words and actions, Jesus makes known the love, holiness, justice, and mercy of God.

The revelation of God through Jesus is comprehensive and transformative. It goes beyond mere intellectual knowledge to a relational understanding of God's heart. By receiving Jesus and believing in His name, individuals are invited into a personal relationship with God, experiencing His love and grace in a profound way.

Becoming Children of God

The Right to Become Children of God

The promise that those who receive Jesus and believe in His name are given the right to become children of God is one of the most profound aspects of the Gospel. This right is not earned but bestowed by grace through faith. It signifies a radical transformation in identity and status.

As children of God, believers are adopted into God's family, enjoying the privileges and responsibilities that come with this new identity. This includes intimate access to the Father, the assurance of His love, and the inheritance of eternal life. Romans 8:15-17 beautifully captures this reality: "The Spirit you received does not make you slaves, so that you live in fear again; rather, the Spirit you received brought about your adoption to sonship. And by him we cry, 'Abba, Father.' The Spirit himself testifies with our spirit that we are God's children. Now if we are children, then we are heirs—heirs of God and co-heirs with Christ, if indeed we share in his sufferings in order that we may also share in his glory."

Born of God

John emphasizes that this new birth is not of natural descent, human decision, or a husband's will, but born of God. This signifies that becoming a child of God is a supernatural act of divine grace. It is not dependent on human effort or lineage but on God's initiative and power.

The concept of being born of God is further explored in John 3:3-8, where Jesus explains to Nicodemus the necessity of being "born again" to see the kingdom of God. This spiritual rebirth is effected by the Holy Spirit, who regenerates and renews believers, making them new creations in Christ.

The Implications for Believers

Living in the Light

As recipients of Jesus' light, believers are called to live in the light. This involves walking in the truth, living according to God's commandments, and reflecting His character in the world. Ephesians 5:8-9 exhorts believers, "For you were once darkness, but now you are light in the Lord. Live as children of light (for the fruit of the light consists in all goodness, righteousness, and truth)."

Living in the light also means rejecting the deeds of darkness and exposing them to the light of God's truth. This involves a commitment to holiness, integrity, and justice, as well as a willingness to bear witness to the transformative power of Jesus in our lives.

Sharing the Light

As followers of Jesus, believers are called to share the light with others. This involves proclaiming the Gospel, demonstrating God's love through acts of compassion and service, and bearing witness to the truth of Jesus. Matthew 5:14-16 highlights this responsibility: "You are the light of the world. A town built on a hill cannot be hidden. Neither do people light a lamp and put it under a bowl. Instead, they put it on its stand, and it gives light to everyone in the house. In the same way, let your light shine before others, that they may see your good deeds and glorify your Father in heaven."

Conclusion

John 1:9-13 reveals the profound truth of Jesus' divine nature as the true light of the world. His coming into the world brings the light of God's truth, illuminating the darkness and offering the promise of becoming children of God to all who receive Him and believe in His name. This revelation invites us into a transformative relationship with

God, marked by the assurance of His love and the call to live and share His light.

As we embrace Jesus as the true light, we are invited to experience the fullness of God's grace and truth, walking in the light and reflecting His character in the world. This foundational understanding of Jesus' divine nature and mission shapes our identity as believers and empowers us to fulfill our calling as children of God. Through Jesus, we encounter the true light that dispels darkness and leads us into the glorious reality of God's kingdom.

Jesus as the Light of the World

In John 8:12, Jesus makes a profound declaration: "I am the light of the world. Whoever follows me will never walk in darkness but will have the light of life." This statement is central to understanding the divine nature of Jesus and His role in bringing spiritual illumination to humanity. In this chapter, we will delve into the significance of this declaration, exploring how Jesus embodies the light of the world and what it means for those who follow Him.

Jesus as the Light of the World

"I am the light of the world..."

The metaphor of light is powerful and deeply rooted in biblical symbolism. Light represents truth, purity, guidance, and the presence of God. By identifying Himself as the light of the world, Jesus asserts His unique role as the source of divine truth and the one who reveals God's presence to humanity.

In the context of John 8, Jesus' declaration follows the Feast of Tabernacles, a Jewish festival that included the lighting of large lamps in the temple courts to commemorate God's guidance of Israel through the wilderness with a pillar of fire. Jesus positions Himself as the fulfillment of this symbolism, claiming to be the ultimate light that guides humanity out of spiritual darkness.

The Divine Nature of Jesus as Light

The Source of Divine Illumination

As the light of the world, Jesus is the source of all spiritual illumination. This role highlights His divine nature, as only God can provide the ultimate revelation of truth and guide people out of darkness. Throughout His ministry, Jesus' teachings and actions revealed the nature of God, corrected misconceptions and provided a path to righteousness.

In John 1:4-5, we read, "In him was life, and that life was the light of all mankind. The light shines in the darkness, and the darkness has not overcome it." This passage underscores the continuous and victorious nature of Jesus' light. Despite the presence of darkness in the world, the light of Jesus remains unextinguished and triumphant.

The Revelation of God

Jesus' role as the light involves revealing the true nature of God. In John 14:9, Jesus says to Philip, "Anyone who has seen me has seen the Father." This statement affirms that Jesus is the visible representation of the invisible God. Through Him, we see the love, holiness, justice, and mercy of God manifested in tangible ways.

The miracles performed by Jesus also serve as revelations of His divine light. Each miracle not only addresses a physical need but also points to a deeper spiritual truth about God's kingdom. For instance, when Jesus heals the blind man in John 9, He declares, "While I am in the world, I am the light of the world" (John 9:5), signifying that His power to restore physical sight is a sign of His ability to illuminate spiritual blindness.

The Call to Follow the Light

"...Whoever follows me will never walk in darkness but will have the light of life."

The promise that those who follow Jesus will never walk in darkness but will have the light of life is both a profound assurance and a call to discipleship. To follow Jesus means to commit to His teachings, embrace His way of life, and walk in His light.

Walking in the light involves living according to the truth revealed by Jesus. It means rejecting the deeds of darkness—sin, falsehood, and moral compromise—and embracing a life of holiness, integrity, and love. Ephesians 5:8-9 exhorts believers, "For you were once darkness, but now you are light in the Lord. Live as children of light (for the fruit of the light consists in all goodness, righteousness, and truth)."

The Light of Life

Eternal and Abundant Life

The "light of life" that Jesus promises to those who follow Him encompasses both eternal life and abundant life here and now. Eternal life refers to the unending fellowship with God that believers will enjoy after this life. Jesus, through His death and resurrection, conquers sin and death, offering eternal life to all who believe in Him.

Abundant life, as described in John 10:10, "I have come that they may have life, and have it to the full," refers to the quality of life that Jesus offers here and now. It is a life characterized by joy, peace, purpose, and the indwelling presence of God. This abundant life is a foretaste of the eternal life to come and is marked by the light of Jesus guiding and transforming every aspect of our existence.

The Implications for Believers
Living in the Light
Believers are called to live in the light of Jesus. This involves daily aligning our lives with His teachings, allowing His truth to guide our decisions and actions. It means being transparent, honest, and walking in integrity, as 1 John 1:7 encourages, "But if we walk in the light, as he is in the light, we have fellowship with one another, and the blood of Jesus, his Son, purifies us from all sin."

Living in the light also means being a light to others. Jesus calls His followers to reflect His light in the world, as seen in Matthew 5:14-16, "You are the light of the world. A town built on a hill cannot be hidden. Neither do people light a lamp and put it under a bowl. Instead, they put it on its stand, and it gives light to everyone in the house. In the same way, let your light shine before others, that they may see your good deeds and glorify your Father in heaven." Believers are to be witnesses to the transformative power of Jesus, bringing His light to dark places and pointing others to Him.

Conclusion
John 8:12 encapsulates the profound truth of Jesus' divine nature as the light of the world. His declaration, "I am the light of the world. Whoever follows me will never walk in darkness but will have the light of life," invites us to embrace Him as the source of divine illumination and the revealer of God's truth. As we follow Jesus, we are called to walk in His light, experiencing the abundant and eternal life He offers and reflecting His light to the world around us.

Understanding Jesus as the light of the world shapes our identity and mission as believers. It calls us to live in the truth, reject darkness, and bearers of His light in a world that desperately needs it. Through Jesus, we encounter the true light that dispels darkness and leads us into the fullness of God's life and love.

CHAPTER 11

JESUS AND THE FATHER ARE ONE

In John 10:30, Jesus makes a profound and provocative statement: "I and the Father are one." This declaration is central to understanding the divine nature of Jesus and His unique relationship with God the Father. It emphasizes the unity and oneness of Jesus with the Father, revealing His divine identity and authority. In this chapter, we will explore the implications of this statement, delving into the theological depth of Jesus' claim and its significance for believers.

The Context of the Declaration

The Good Shepherd

The context of John 10:30 is Jesus' discourse on being the Good Shepherd. In John 10:11, Jesus says, "I am the good shepherd. The good shepherd lays down his life for the sheep." Throughout this passage, Jesus contrasts Himself with the hired hand who does not care for the sheep. He emphasizes His deep commitment to His flock, willing to sacrifice His life for their well-being.

In John 10:27-29, just before declaring His oneness with the Father, Jesus speaks about His sheep hearing His voice, following Him, and receiving eternal life. He assures them that no one can snatch them out of His hand, and then extends this assurance to the Father's protection: "My Father, who has given them to me, is greater than all; no one can snatch them out of my Father's hand." This sets the stage for His statement of unity with the Father.

The Declaration of Oneness

"I and the Father are one."

When Jesus declares, "I and the Father are one," He is affirming a profound theological truth about His divine nature and relationship with God the Father. This statement underscores several key aspects of His identity:

1. Unity of Essence: Jesus is claiming that He and the Father are one in essence and nature. This goes beyond mere agreement or harmony; it speaks to a shared divine substance. Jesus is affirming that He is fully God, co-equal with the Father in all aspects of His being.

2. Unity of Purpose: Jesus' mission is in complete alignment with the Father's will. Throughout His ministry, Jesus repeatedly emphasizes that He came to do the Father's will (John 6:38). Their unity is demonstrated in their shared purpose of salvation and the protection of believers.

3. Divine Authority: By claiming oneness with the Father, Jesus is asserting His divine authority. This authority is evident in His power to grant eternal life and protect His sheep from any force that might seek to harm them.

The Reaction of the Jewish Leaders

Hostility and Accusations

The Jewish leaders' reaction to Jesus' declaration reveals the gravity of His claim. In John 10:31-33, we read,

"Again his Jewish opponents picked up stones to stone him, but Jesus said to them, 'I have shown you many good works from the Father. For which of these do you stone me?' 'We are not stoning you for any good work,' they replied, 'but for blasphemy, because you, a mere man, claim to be God.'"

The leaders understood that Jesus was claiming equality with God, which they considered blasphemy. Their intent to stone Him underscores the seriousness with which they viewed His statement. This reaction also highlights the radical nature of Jesus' identity and mission, which challenged the established religious norms and expectations.

Theological Implications of Oneness

The Trinity

Jesus' declaration of oneness with the Father is foundational to the Christian doctrine of the Trinity. The Trinity is the belief in one God who exists in three distinct persons: the Father, the Son (Jesus Christ), and the Holy Spirit. Each person is fully God, sharing the same divine essence, yet distinct in their personhood and roles.

The concept of the Trinity is a mystery that transcends human understanding, but it is essential for grasping the full revelation of God's nature. Jesus' claim to be one with the Father affirms His place within the Trinity and underscores the unity and diversity within the Godhead.

Revelation of God's Nature

Through His unity with the Father, Jesus reveals the nature and character of God. In John 14:9, Jesus tells Philip, "Anyone who has seen me has seen the Father." This statement underscores that Jesus' life, teachings, and actions are the perfect representation of God's nature. In Him, we see God's love, compassion, holiness, and truth made manifest.

This revelation invites believers into a deeper relationship with God. By knowing Jesus, we come to know the Father more intimately. Jesus bridges the gap between the divine and human, providing a way for us to experience the fullness of God's presence and love.

The Assurance for Believers

Eternal Security

Jesus' unity with the Father provides profound assurance for believers. In John 10:28-29, He promises eternal security for His sheep: "I give them eternal life, and they shall never perish; no one will snatch them out of my hand. My Father, who has given them to me, is greater than all; no one can snatch them out of my Father's hand."

This assurance is rooted in the divine power and faithfulness of both the Father and the Son. Believers can trust in their eternal security, knowing that their salvation is upheld by the omnipotent God. This promise is a source of comfort and strength, especially in times of trial and uncertainty.

Unity in the Body of Christ

Jesus' unity with the Father also has implications for the unity of His followers. In His high priestly prayer, Jesus prays for the unity of believers: "I pray also for those who will believe in me through their message, that all of them may be one, Father, just as you are in me and I am in you" (John 17:20-21).

This prayer underscores the importance of unity within the body of Christ. As believers, we are called to reflect the unity of the Father and the Son in our relationships with one another. This unity is a powerful testimony to the world of God's love and the truth of the Gospel.

Conclusion

John 10:30 encapsulates a profound truth about Jesus' divine nature and His unique relationship with the Father: "I and the Father are one." This statement reveals the unity of essence, purpose, and authority between Jesus and the Father, affirming His deity and His role within the Trinity.

Understanding Jesus' oneness with the Father deepens our appreciation of His mission and the assurance He provides to believers. It invites us into a transformative relationship with God, where we experience His love, security, and unity. As we follow Jesus, we are called to reflect His unity with the Father in our lives, demonstrating the reality of His divine nature to the world.

This foundational truth shapes our identity and mission as followers of Christ, empowering us to live in the light of His presence and to share the hope and love of the Gospel with others. Through Jesus, we encounter the fullness of God's revelation, experiencing the profound reality of His oneness and the transformative power of His love.

Jesus and the Father Are One

In John 14:9-11, Jesus makes a profound statement that affirms His divine identity and unity with God the Father: "Jesus answered: 'Don't you know me, Philip, even after I have been among you such a long time? Anyone who has seen me has seen the Father. How can you say, 'Show us the Father'? Don't you believe that I am in the Father, and that the Father is in me? The words I say to you I do not speak on my own authority. Rather, it is the Father, living in me, who is doing his work. Believe me when I say that I am in the Father and the Father is in me; or at least believe on the evidence of the works themselves.'" This passage provides a clear and compelling insight into the divine nature of Jesus and His intimate relationship with the Father. In this chapter, we will delve into the significance of Jesus' words, exploring how they reveal His divine identity and unity with God.

The Context of Jesus' Declaration

The Upper Room Discourse

The setting of John 14 is the Upper Room, where Jesus is sharing a final meal with His disciples before His arrest and crucifixion. This section of John's Gospel, often referred to as the Upper Room Discourse, contains some of Jesus' most intimate and profound teachings. It is here that He seeks to prepare His disciples for the coming trials and to reassure them of His continuing presence and guidance.

Philip's Request

In John 14:8, Philip makes a request: "Lord, show us the Father and that will be enough for us." This request reflects a deep longing to see and know God more fully. Jesus' response to Philip's request forms the basis of His profound declaration about His unity with the Father.

Jesus Reveals the Father

"Anyone who has seen me has seen the Father."

Jesus' statement, "Anyone who has seen me has seen the Father," is a direct assertion of His divine identity. He is not merely a representative of God or a prophet; He is the exact representation of God. This claim underscores that Jesus embodies the fullness of God's nature and character. To see Jesus is to see God Himself.

In Colossians 1:15, the Apostle Paul echoes this truth: "The Son is the image of the invisible God, the firstborn over all creation." Jesus makes the invisible God visible, revealing God's love, holiness, compassion, and truth in a way that is accessible and comprehensible to humanity.

The Unity of Jesus and the Father

Jesus continues, "Don't you believe that I am in the Father, and that the Father is in me?" This rhetorical question emphasizes the profound unity between Jesus and the Father. Their relationship is characterized by mutual indwelling, where Jesus is in the Father and the Father is in Jesus. This unity goes beyond a mere agreement of purpose or mission; it speaks to an essential oneness in their divine nature.

This mutual indwelling is a mystery that points to the doctrine of the Trinity, where the Father, Son, and Holy Spirit are distinct persons yet one in essence. The unity between Jesus and the Father highlights the co-equality and co-eternity of the Son with the Father, affirming His full divinity.

The Authority and Works of Jesus

"The words I say to you I do not speak on my own authority. Rather, it is the Father, living in me, who is doing his work."

Jesus explains that His words and works are not done on His own authority but are a direct expression of the Father's will and power. This statement underscores the intimate cooperation and harmony between Jesus and the Father. Every word Jesus speaks and every miracle He performs are manifestations of the Father's presence and activity through Him.

This assertion challenges any notion that Jesus acts independently of the Father. Instead, it reveals that Jesus' ministry is a perfect reflection of the Father's will. His teachings, miracles, and actions are direct revelations of God's character and purposes.

Evidence of the Works

Jesus urges His disciples to believe in His unity with the Father based on the evidence of His works: "Believe me when I say that I am in the Father and the Father is in me; or at least believe on the evidence of the works themselves." The miracles Jesus performed—healing the sick, raising the dead, feeding the multitudes, and calming the storm—are not just displays of power but signs that reveal His divine identity and the Father's presence in Him.

These works are consistent with the nature and mission of God as revealed in the Old Testament. They point to Jesus as the fulfillment of God's promises and the embodiment of His redemptive work. The miracles are tangible proof that Jesus is who He claims to be—the Son of God, one with the Father.

Theological Implications of Jesus' Unity with the Father

The Revelation of God

Jesus' unity with the Father is foundational to the Christian understanding of God. Through Jesus, we gain the fullest and most direct revelation of God's nature. Hebrews 1:1-3 states, "In the past God spoke to our ancestors through the prophets at many times and in various ways, but in these last days he has spoken to us by his Son, whom he appointed heir of all things, and through whom also he made the universe. The Son is the radiance of God's glory and the exact representation of his being, sustaining all things by his powerful word."

This revelation is not merely informational but relational. Jesus invites us to know God personally and intimately, experiencing His love, grace, and truth in our lives. Through Jesus, we are brought into a relationship with the Father, transforming our understanding of God from a distant deity to a loving Father.

The Assurance of Salvation

Jesus' unity with the Father provides the basis for the assurance of our salvation. As the one who perfectly reveals the Father and accomplishes His will, Jesus is uniquely qualified to be our Savior. His sacrificial death and resurrection are the ultimate expressions of the Father's love and justice, securing our redemption and reconciliation with God.

John 14:6 underscores this assurance: "Jesus answered, 'I am the way and the truth and the life. No one comes to the Father except through me.'" Jesus is the exclusive and sufficient means of salvation, providing a secure and unchanging foundation for our faith.

The Call to Reflect Jesus' Unity with the Father

Living in Union with Christ

Believers are called to live in union with Christ, reflecting His unity with the Father in our lives. This involves abiding in Jesus, allowing His words and Spirit to transform us and guide our actions. John 15:4-5 emphasizes this relationship: "Remain in me, as I also remain in you. No branch can bear fruit by itself; it must remain in the vine. Neither can you bear fruit unless you remain in me. I am the vine; you are the branches. If you remain in me and I in you, you will bear much fruit; apart from me you can do nothing."

Living in union with Christ means cultivating a deep and abiding relationship with Him, characterized by prayer, obedience, and dependence on His grace. As we remain in Him, His life flows through us, producing spiritual fruit and reflecting the Father's character to the world.

Witnessing to the World

Jesus' unity with the Father also compels us to witness to the world. Just as Jesus revealed the Father through His words and works, we are called to reveal Jesus through our lives. This involves sharing the Gospel, demonstrating God's love through acts of compassion and justice, and living in a way that reflects the values of God's kingdom.

Matthew 5:14-16 captures this calling: "You are the light of the world. A town built on a hill cannot be hidden. Neither do people light a lamp and put it under a bowl. Instead they put it on its stand, and it gives light to everyone in the house. In the same way, let your light shine before others, that they may see your good deeds and glorify your Father in heaven."

Conclusion

John 14:9-11 reveals the profound truth of Jesus' divine nature and His unique unity with the Father. His declaration that anyone who has seen Him has seen the Father underscores His role as the ultimate revelation of God. Through His words and works, Jesus makes the Father's presence and character known, inviting us into a transformative relationship with God.

Understanding Jesus' unity with the Father deepens our faith and assures us of our salvation. It calls us to live in union with Christ, reflecting His character and mission in our lives. As we abide in Him and bear witness to His truth, we participate in the ongoing revelation of God's love and grace to the world.

This foundational truth shapes our identity as believers and empowers us to fulfill our calling as ambassadors of Christ. Through Jesus, we encounter the fullness of God's revelation, experiencing the profound reality of His oneness and the transformative power of His love.

Why is Christmas on December 25?